Florida's Unexpected Wildlife

UNIVERSITY PRESS OF FLORIDA

Florida A&M University, Tallahassee
Florida Atlantic University, Boca Raton
Florida Gulf Coast University, Ft. Myers
Florida International University, Miami
Florida State University, Tallahassee
New College of Florida, Sarasota
University of Central Florida, Orlando
University of Florida, Gainesville
University of North Florida, Jacksonville
University of South Florida, Tampa
University of West Florida, Pensacola

University Press of Florida
Gainesville · Tallahassee · Tampa · Boca Raton · Pensacola
Orlando · Miami · Jacksonville · Ft. Myers · Sarasota

Florida's Unexpected Wildlife

Exotic Species, Living Fossils, and Mythical Beasts
in the Sunshine State

MICHAEL NEWTON

12 11 10 09 08 07   6 5 4 3 2 1

Library of Congress Cataloging-in-Publication Data
Newton, Michael, 1951–
Florida's unexpected wildlife : exotic species, living fossils, and
mythical beasts in the Sunshine State / Michael Newton.
p. cm.
Includes bibliographical references and index.
ISBN 978-0-8130-3156-9 (alk. paper)
   1. Monsters—Florida. 2. Living fossils—Florida.
3. Animals, Mythical—Florida. I. Title.
QL89.N55   2007
591.9759—dc22   2007007771

The University Press of Florida is the scholarly publishing
agency for the State University System of Florida, comprising
Florida A&M University, Florida Atlantic University, Florida
Gulf Coast University, Florida International University, Florida
State University, New College of Florida, University of Central
Florida, University of Florida, University of North Florida,
University of South Florida, and University of West Florida.

University Press of Florida
15 Northwest 15th Street
Gainesville, FL 32611-2079
http://www.upf.com

In memory of J. Richard Greenwell

Contents

Preface

The Crypto-Zoo

In 1957, Belgian zoologist Bernard Heuvelmans coined the term
cryptozoology, subsequently defined as "the scientific study of hidden animals, i.e., of still unknown animal forms about which only testimonial or circumstantial evidence is available, or material evidence considered insufficient by some." When the International Society of Cryptozoology was organized in 1982, with Heuvelmans as president, the founders proclaimed that cryptozoology also concerns "the possible existence of *known* animals in areas where they are not supposed to occur (either now or in the past) as well as the unknown persistence of presumed extinct animals to the present time or to the recent past. . . . What makes an animal of interest to cryptozoology . . . is that it is *unexpected.*"[1]

Hidden or unexpected animals are not "unknown," as some authors persist in claiming; rather, we may say that their existence in most cases is officially unverified. Likewise, most do not qualify for the derogatory "monster" label frequently applied to any creature presently unclassified by science. John Wall, writing to the ISC's

Giant anacondas are reported periodically from the Amazon jungle. (Copyright William Rebsamen.)

quarterly newsletter in 1983, proposed the alternative label *cryptid* ("hidden animal"), which is used throughout this text.[2]

In 1985, ISC Secretary J. Richard Greenwell proposed a classification system for cryptids, including the following groups:[3]

(1) Members of a known, living species whose form, size, color, or pattern is extraordinary for its species (for example, reports of giant anacondas in Brazil).

(2) Extant and well-known species unrecognized as living in a particular area (for example, kangaroos in North America).

(3) Presumably extinct species, not fossil forms, known only from limited organic evidence (skin, feathers, and so on) but without a complete type specimen (the original specimen used to classify a new species).

(4) Known species presumed extinct within historical times, which may have survived to the present day (for example, Australian thylacines, also called Tasmanian tigers).

(5) Representatives of fossil forms presumed extinct during geologic times, which may have survived into historical times or to the present day (for example, the coelacanth, representing lobe-finned fishes previously known only from fossils).

(6) New species such as the Yeti, known from anecdotal evidence, for which no known organic evidence exists.

(7) New species previously unreported or else known only to aboriginal people, which may be accidentally discovered and accepted by zoologists (for example, the megamouth shark).

Florida's Unexpected Wildlife reviews, for the first time in book form, the history and broad scope of cryptozoology in Florida. It does not, as Dr. Heuvelmans declared in 1982, present "an arcane or occult zoology."[4] Nothing within these pages shall pertain to aliens from outer space or any aspect of the supernatural. That said, however, there is no shortage of mysteries to be explored.

Florida's Unexpected Wildlife consists of nine chapters, topically arranged. Chapter 1 examines Florida's "naturalized" exotic ani-

Numerous modern witnesses describe encounters with living thylacines in Australia. (Copyright William Rebsamen.)

mals, introduced species of which some are now fully recognized by science as members of the state's fauna. Chapter 2 reviews the evidence for "living fossils" in the Sunshine State. Chapter 3 presents accounts of "sea serpents" from the Atlantic coast and Gulf of Mexico. Chapter 4 considers the ongoing debate over alleged remains of an unclassified giant octopus, stranded at St. Augustine in 1896. Chapter 5 introduces the state's freshwater cryptids, commonly described as "lake monsters" or "river monsters." Chapter 6 dissects the 1948 case of Clearwater's "Three-Toes," with media assertions of a hoax published in 1988. Chapter 7 surveys Florida reports of exotic or nonnative big cats, including lions and "black panthers." Chapter 8 summarizes the controversy surrounding "skunk apes," from Seminole legends to the "Myakka photos" of the year 2000 and beyond. Chapter 9 collects loose ends, including eyewitness reports of giant birds and armadillos, pink alligators, elusive kangaroos, and the predatory Chupacabra or "goat sucker." A conclusion discusses the likelihood of finding new or unexpected animals in Florida during the new millennium.

I owe a debt of gratitude to several people, without whom the work in hand might not exist. Editor John Byram's support at UPF was essential and is much appreciated. Veteran cryptozoologist Loren Coleman and artist Bill Rebsamen provided unique illustrations for the text. Valuable information for various chapters was furnished by Susan Abbott, National Archives and Records Administration; Holly Beasley and Kathy Mays, Jacksonville's Beaches Area Historical Society; Nelda Caldwell, Florida Fish and Wildlife Conservation Commission; cryptozoologist Mark Hall; Diana Harris, *Englewood Sun;* Linda Ramsey, *Pensacola News Journal;* Bob Silkett, Jacksonville Public Library; Bernard Unti, Humane Society of the United States; Nan Weaver, Escambia County Sheriff's Department; and Cindy West, Pensacola Police Department. And as always, my wife, Heather, was supportive far above and beyond the call of spousal duty. Readers wishing to report encounters with Florida cryptids are invited to contact me, either through UPF or directly via my Web site, at http://www.michaelnewton.homestead. com.

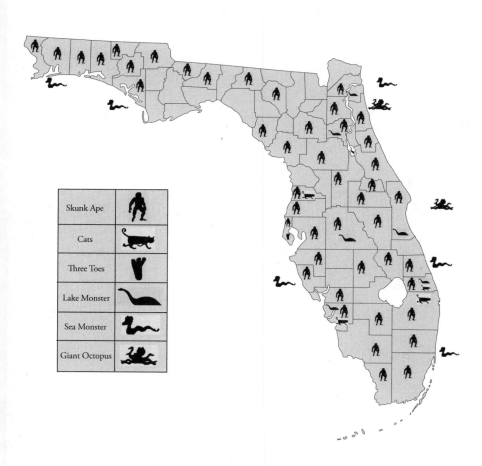

Skunk Ape	
Cats	
Three Toes	
Lake Monster	
Sea Monster	
Giant Octopus	

Uninvited Guests

Florida's hospitable climate constantly lures new species to colonize the Sunshine State. *Homo sapiens* has had the most profound environmental impact on the region, but humans are not alone on the state's list of exotic (nonnative) species; the others range from tiny insects to authentically "giant" reptiles—and, perhaps, a few species as yet unclassified.

According to Florida's Fish and Wildlife Conservation Commission (FWCC), 279 exotic species have been cataloged in the state since 1875, although 44 of those species officially have "no current population." Inspectors list 128 exotic species breeding in the wild, with 27 expanding, 10 stable, and 8 species declining. A total of 189 species have unknown population levels.[1] The success of so many "naturalized" species suggests that others, presently unlisted by the FWCC, also may be present.

Birds

The FWCC acknowledges 157 exotic bird species presently living in Florida, with at least 48 species breeding in the wild (though only 11 species rank as "established").[2] One species missing from that roster is the Australian emu (*Dromaius novaehollandiae*) that sparked a furor in Pensacola during autumn 2003.

Steve Massey was jogging through the Little Creek subdivision on October 17, 2003, when he sighted a six-foot-tall emu strutting through some nearby shrubbery. Massey reported the encounter to police, who acknowledged the recent escape of an emu named Clyde from DeFuniak Springs, but Clyde's owner announced that the errant emu was recaptured on October 16, the day before Massey's sighting. Diane Norris, animal curator at The Zoo, near Gulf Breeze, noted the presence of several emu farms in the district, but none reported any missing birds. At press time for this volume, the Pensacola emu had not reappeared, nor had authorities logged any word of an escape.[3]

Mammals

The FWCC lists twenty-seven species of exotic mammals presently living in Florida, with all but six species successfully breeding in the wild. The invaders range in size from rats to elk and include three species of monkeys. Rhesus monkeys (*Macaca mulatta*) colonized Florida in 1930, while vervet monkeys (*Chlorocebus aethiops*) and squirrel monkeys (*Saimiri sciureus*) arrived in the 1950s and 1960s, respectively.[4]

Like most other exotic species in Florida, monkeys were introduced by humans, either as private pets or as an adjunct to the tourist industry. Rhesus monkeys got their foothold at Silver Springs in 1930, when a small group was imported to amuse vacationing tourists. Some subsequently fled their cages or were freed deliberately, and these established breeding colonies. Sporadic sightings continue in the twenty-first century, including a spate of reports from Wekiwa Springs State Park, logged between June 2002 and November 2003.[5]

Reptiles

State inspectors recognize forty-eight species of exotic reptiles in Florida, forty-five of them with breeding populations in the wild.

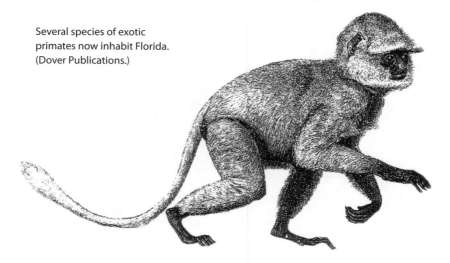

Several species of exotic
primates now inhabit Florida.
(Dover Publications.)

Their number officially includes one turtle, one crocodilian, four
snakes, and forty-four lizards of various sizes. The spectacled caiman (*Caiman crocodilus*), established in South Florida since 1960,
may pass on casual inspection for a native alligator, but other naturalized reptiles persistently startle witnesses with their size and/or
alien appearance.[6]

Lizards at large in Florida include three species of iguanas, ranging in length from three to six feet. The largest species, established
in the Keys since 1966, is the green iguana (*Iguana iguana*), reported
as thriving by the "hundreds, maybe thousands." In March 2003,
FWCC spokesman Chris Bergh told reporters, "There is plenty of
evidence that they are causing problems in people's residential and
commercial landscapes, just from the destruction of vegetation."
One case in point was a butterfly garden at Blue Hole Park on Big
Pine Key, where green iguanas "moved in and ate pretty much everything." On Florida's mainland, populations of Mexican spinytail
iguanas (*Ctenosaura pectinata*) and black spinytail iguanas (*C. si-
milis*) established themselves by 1972 and 1978, respectively. Unlike
the herbivorous green iguana, both species include eggs and small
vertebrates in their diet, threatening sea turtle hatchlings and various nesting birds.[7]

More intimidating still is the Nile monitor (*Varanus niloticus*),
an omnivorous African lizard that may reach nearly seven feet in

Two exotic species of iguanas are presently thriving in Florida. (Dover Publications.)

length. FWCC spokesmen list the Nile monitor's "first year" in Florida as 1990, but other sources tell a different story.[8] Published accounts describe captures of at least four large monitors, spanning eleven years prior to the breeding population's official launch date. They include a specimen caught outside South Bay in 1979; a six-foot-five-inch monitor captured on a golf course at Royal Palm Beach on June 21, 1981; a five-foot specimen snared in North Miami on July 14, 1981; and another of equal size caught at Hypoluxo one day later.[9] By June 2004, an estimated five hundred to one thousand monitors inhabited Cape Coral alone, prompting the National Fish and Wildlife Foundation to launch a $52,000 eradication project.[10]

Few creatures inspire more revulsion in humans than snakes, and while the FWCC recognizes only three exotic species established in Florida, two—the common boa (*Boa constrictor*) and the Burmese python (*Python molurus bivitattus*)—rank among the largest in the world.[11]

State spokesmen date the python's arrival from the 1980s, and the boa's from 1990, but tales of huge snakes dwelling in the Everglades have circulated since the nineteenth century, gleaned from Seminole accounts. It seems unlikely that captive pythons were common in Florida during that era, but it is estimated that in August 1992 more than one thousand pet snakes allegedly escaped from their owners during Hurricane Andrew. By May 2004, sixty-seven Burmese pythons were killed or captured in Everglades National Park, while a twenty-foot specimen was caught in Kendall and a sixteen-footer was bagged at Vero Beach in July 2004. Two incidents in October 2005 reminded South Floridians once more of their exotic neighbors. In northwest Miami–Dade County, a ten-foot python devoured an eighteen-pound cat in a residential neighborhood, while a thirteen-foot Everglades specimen burst after swallowing a six-foot alligator.[12]

The anaconda (*Eunectes murinus*), a staple monster of pulp fiction and modern horror films, does not appear on any roster of Florida's known exotics, but at least one specimen apparently made its home in Cady's Cove, near the mouth of the Kissimmee River, in the 1990s. Fishing guide Tom Frates made several attempts to kill the "huge, colorful serpent," but his gunshots always missed their mark, leaving the reptile unscathed—and, perhaps, still living.[13] Indeed, in a climate where Asian pythons and South American boas

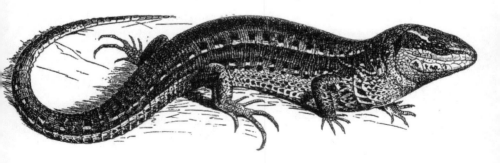

Old World monitor lizards have also colonized parts of southern Florida. (Dover Publications.)

thrive, there seems to be no reason why anacondas should not do equally as well.

Two nineteenth-century tales of giant snakes also deserve inclusion here. The first, reported in November 1878, involves a Mr. Long of Brevard County, described as "one of the most reliable men of this section." While driving his oxcart near Fort Drum, long saw a huge rattlesnake and killed it with his whip, after an exhausting struggle. Measuring the carcass with his eighteen-foot whip, Long determined that it was approximately fifteen feet, six inches long. Its body was "as large around as a big blue bucket," and its rattle included thirty-nine segments. America's largest known rattler, the eastern diamondback (*Crotalus adamanteus*) does not officially exceed eight feet in length.[14]

An equally strange report emerged from Orange County in September 1887. An unnamed farmer living near Orlando allegedly surprised a huge snake feeding on a rabbit and allowed it to finish before moving closer with his gun. As he approached, the snake raised its head "as high as a good sized man," then "began racing back and forth before him, drawing nearer each time, hissing and darting out its tongue." The farmer fired in self-defense, afterward measuring the carcass at sixteen feet long, with a head four inches wide. Published accounts describe it as "a 'coachwhip' snake, of the boa constrictor family." In fact, Florida's eastern coachwhip snake (*Masticophis flagellum flagellum*) is completely unrelated to the boas and attains a maximum official length of five feet. Various Latin American boas may reach the size described and survive in Florida's climate, but their behavior does not typically match that of the serpent in question.[15]

Fish

Fish do not rate as "wildlife" on the FWCC's wildlife roster, but the agency maintains a separate list of eighteen exotic species presently breeding in Florida lakes and rivers.[16] The most unusual of those—the gluttonous, air-breathing bullseye snakehead (*Channa marulius*)—has featured in two recent horror films, but its public

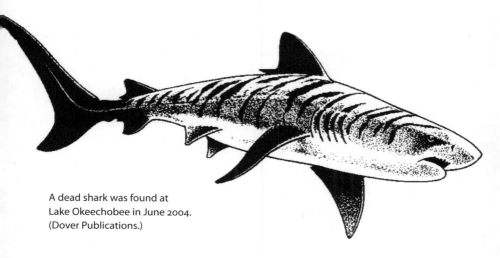

A dead shark was found at
Lake Okeechobee in June 2004.
(Dover Publications.)

recognition factor pales beside that of the South American piranha.

Piranhas rank with sharks among the world's most notorious fish. Science recognizes ten species, all legally banned from importation to Florida, where authorities recognize the possibility of an established colony. Nonetheless, a breeding population of green tiger piranhas (*Serrasalmus humeralis*) survived in a display pool at Miami's Monkey Jungle amusement park through September 1977. Individual captures are also reported from Miami's Snapper Creek, from Boca Raton's Lake Mabo (where authorities poisoned all fish in the lake during April 1979), and from a canal west of Fort Lauderdale. Reports of multiple piranhas pulled from the Tamiami Canal during 1969–79 remain unconfirmed.[17]

Florida's strangest fish story emerged from Lake Okeechobee in the third week of June 2004. Local resident Mario Rodriguez was walking along the lake's northern shoreline when he found a shark at least four feet long, lying dead at the water's edge. Unnamed officials subsequently told reporters that the fish was "either a nurse shark dumped in the lake or a bull shark," the latter "known to travel many miles inland in freshwater." Several canals link Lake

Okeechobee to the Atlantic, while the Caloosahatchee River runs from Okeechobee (via Lake Hicpochee) to the Gulf of Mexico, yet the anonymous pundits seemed uncomfortable with their own explanation of the shark's demise. "How it got there," they concluded on June 25, "remains a mystery."[18]

The Wild Unknown

If the FWCC acknowledges 235 exotic wildlife species and 18 exotic freshwater fish now established in Florida, what else may we expect to find within the Sunshine State? Has any other species of substantial size slipped through the net? Is there a possibility that creatures deemed extinct may still survive? And what of transient visitors from other states—or from the sea? Does modern Florida support species unknown to science, or should we dismiss all such reports as flights of fantasy?

Die-hard believers and debunkers never will agree on answers to those questions, because they will not give an inch in their debate over the mysteries of nature. With tolerance and perseverance, however, we may find a middle ground between the two extremes. And if the "final truth" is not discovered there, at least we may enjoy the quest.

Going ... Going ... Gone?

Extinction, whether prompted by natural selection or the thought-less acts of humankind, marks the termination of a species. From geologic times to the twenty-first century, thousands of species have vanished from Earth, swept away for all time, leaving only their fossil remains, preserved relics, or photos to prove that they ever existed.

Cryptozoologists, however, are sometimes reluctant to accept "extinction" as the final word. Their quest for "living fossils"—crea-tures that defy scholarly efforts to erase them from the list of extant species—spans the globe. Some famous (or notorious) examples include *Mokele-mbembe,* a relict dinosaur alleged by some to dwell in certain Congo basin backwaters; surviving plesiosaurs, supposed by some to dwell in lakes ranging from Scotland to Argentina; and Australia's thylacine, a doglike marsupial predator officially extinct since the 1930s.[1]

While none of those elusive cryptids has been found alive so far, some living fossils *have* surprised researchers by appearing in the modern world, alive and well. A classic case (and "poster child" for cryptozoology) is the coelacanth (*Latimera chalumnae*), a lobe-finned fish first identified from fossil remains in 1836, presumed

Reports of living dinosaurs still emerge from Africa's Congo basin.
(Copyright William Rebsamen.)

by paleontologists to have vanished from Earth some sixty-five million years ago. That assumption proved false in December 1938, when fishermen delivered a freshly caught coelacanth to market at East London, South Africa. Museum curator Marjorie Courtenay-Latimer claimed the specimen, which was subsequently identified by ichthyologist J. L. B. Smith. Another fourteen years elapsed before a second specimen was caught off Comoros, in December 1952, but by 1975, an additional 203 coelacanths had been hauled from the depths. The German naturalist Hans Fricke photographed six living specimens off Grand Comoro Island in 1987, and another coelacanth population was reported from Indonesian waters in September 1997.[2]

In short, the experts had been wrong.

Many other "resurrections" from presumed extinction may be cited, including the pacarana (1904), Morelet's crocodile (1923), the golden hamster (1930), the desert rat kangaroo (1931), Cabanis's tanager (1937), the pygmy killer whale (1954), James's flamingo

(1956), Fraser's dolphin (1956), the wood bison (1957), Bolsón's tortoise (1959), the Seychelles scops owl (1959), Leadbeater's opossum (1961), the black-footed ferret (1964), the parma wallaby and white-throated wallaby (1965), the long-footed potoroo (1967), the pygmy hog (1971), the yellow-tailed woolly monkey (1974), Ridley's roundleaf bat (1975), Andrews's beaked whale (1976), Bulmer's fruit bat (1980), the Deniliquen wombat (1985), the Javan rhinoceros (1988), the Chinese otter (1990), the desert warthog (1991), the bay cat (1992), Roosevelt's muntjac (1995), the Barbary lion (1996), and the dusky hopping mouse (2003), among others.[3]

While yet undocumented, Florida allegedly plays host to several species listed as extinct. They are examined in this chapter with the anecdotal evidence for their survival.

The Carolina Parakeet

The Carolina parakeet (*Conuropsis carolinensis*), initially described in 1891, was North America's only indigenous member of the parrot family (*Pittacidae*). Although a small bird, it was noteworthy for brilliant plumage, including a yellow head and orange face, and was

Although presumed extinct for sixty-five million years, the coelacanth was found alive and well in 1938. (Copyright William Rebsamen.)

Some witnesses assert that the Carolina parakeet is not extinct. (Dover Publications.)

bright green overall. Its native range spanned Florida, Georgia, and South Carolina, wherein its frugivorous diet drove farmers with orchards to kill the birds on sight. The birds surviving that slaughter were trapped for sale as pets or were killed for use as ornaments on women's hats. The last confirmed wild specimens were shot at Lake Okeechobee in April 1904, while the last captive specimen—a male named Incas—died at the Cincinnati Zoo on February 21, 1918.[4]

Although officially extinct, Carolina parakeets were still reported from the wild over the next two decades. In 1920, witness Henry

Redding claimed a sighting of thirty parakeets along Fort Drum Creek, in Okeechobee County. Six years later, also in Okeechobee County, Charles Doe saw three pairs of the elusive birds and collected several of their eggs, which he preserved as evidence. Bird wardens employed by the National Audubon Society reported multiple sightings of green parakeets with yellow heads from South Carolina's Santee Swamp (in Sumter County), during the 1930s, but those claims did not prevent workmen from draining the swamp in 1938, to construct the Santee-Cooper Hydroelectric Project. Meanwhile, bird-watcher Oren Stemville made a color motion-picture film of a still-unidentified parakeet during 1937, in Georgia's Okefenokee Swamp.[5]

No sightings of a Carolina parakeet in Florida have been reported publicly since 1926, and while they may still theoretically exist, any future sightings will be complicated by the FWCC's listing of sixteen exotic parakeet species sighted in Florida between 1920 and 1987. None are listed as established in the state, and one—the orange-fronted parakeet (*Aratinga canicularis*)—was officially extirpated soon after its 1972 arrival, but fifteen species remain present in unknown numbers. Possible look-alikes for the Carolina parakeet include the green parakeet (*A. holochlora*), reported first in 1920, and the red-masked parakeet (*A. erthogenys*), both of which have been breeding in the wild for "at least ten years" but are still "not established" to official satisfaction. Other parakeets known to inhabit the Florida wilds include the blue-crowned (*A. acuticaudata*), brown-throated (*A. pertinax*), crimson-fronted (*A. finschi*), dusky-headed (*A. weddellii*), Hispaniolan (*A. chloroptera*), mitred (*A. mitrata*), orange-chinned (*Brotogeris jugularis*), peach-fronted (*A. aurea*), scarlet-fronted (*A. wagleri*), tui (*B. sanctithomae*), white-eyed (*A. leucopthalmus*), white-winged (*B. versicolurus*), and yellow-chevroned (*B. chiriri*).[6]

The Ivory-Billed Woodpecker

North America's largest woodpecker, the ivory-billed, was christened *Campephilus principalis principalis* by Carl von Linné in 1758, then received the alternate name *C. p. bairdii* from John Cassin in

The "extinct" ivory-billed woodpecker was found alive in Arkansas, in April 2005. (From author's collection.)

1863, based on specimens obtained from Cuba. Stateside observers nicknamed it the "Lord God Bird," after the startled exclamations voiced by witnesses upon their first encounter with a twenty-inch woodpecker displaying black-and-white plumage (with a bright crimson crest on male specimens). Its white bill instantly distinguished the ivory-bill from the otherwise similar, but slightly smaller, pileated woodpecker (*Dryocopus pileatus*).[7]

The ivory-billed woodpecker once ranged throughout Dixie, from North Carolina to eastern Texas, and northward through the Mississippi River valley to Missouri, southern Illinois, and Indiana. It was, sadly, another avian victim of man's depredations, needlessly slaughtered by hunters, while commercial logging eradicated much of its natural forest habitat. The last confirmed sighting of an ivory-bill in Florida dates from 1924, when a specimen was shot near Tallahassee and was sold for $150 to the University of Florida. Nationwide, the last confirmed sighting of the twentieth century was recorded in 1944. The species was officially presumed extinct in mainland North America by the early 1960s, and in Cuba by 1990.[8]

Still, as in the case of the Carolina parakeet and so many other lost species, sightings continued. Wildlife artist Frank Shields reported sightings of single specimens near Interlachen, Florida, on April 4 and 15, 1969, followed by the recovery of a distinctive black-and-white feather from the same region on June 11, 1969. Elsewhere across the southern United States, tentative sightings were filed by John Dennis in Texas (1966–67), by a Louisiana bird-watcher (1971), and by Louisiana zoologist David Kulivan (1999). "Earwitness" reports of the ivory-bill's distinctive rapping sounds also emerged from Mississippi (1987) and from Louisiana's Pearl River Wildlife Management Area (1999). Members of a subsequent Louisiana expedition recorded presumed woodpecker tapping sounds in 2002, but ornithologists at Cornell University dismissed the sounds as distant gunfire.[9]

Ironically, it was another Cornell spokesperson who broke the stunning news, in April 2005, that ivory-billed woodpeckers had been found alive and well in the Big Woods region of eastern Arkansas. As detailed in the Cornell report, a yearlong expedition including fifty members, operating under quasi-military security precautions, produced multiple eyewitness sightings and caught at least one ivory-bill on videotape. John Fitzpatrick, director of the Cornell Laboratory of Ornithology, declared, "The bird captured on video is clearly an ivory-billed woodpecker. Amazingly, America may have another chance to protect the future of this spectacular bird and the awesome forests in which it lives." Scott Simon, director of the Nature Conservancy's Arkansas branch, agreed. "It is a landmark rediscovery," he said. "Finding the ivory-bill in Arkansas validates decades of great conservation work and represents an incredible story of hope for the future."[10]

Rediscovery of the ivory-billed woodpecker, while clearly not on par with capture of a living coelacanth, whose closest relatives were thought to have disappeared during the Cretaceous period, energized bird-watchers and cryptozoologists alike. It also, predictably, inspired a rash of sightings from Virginia to South Daytona, Florida, where John Hicks allegedly saw an ivory-bill with a "huge wingspan" at the Ra-Mar mobile home park. It was, Hicks assured reporters, "the one y'all wrote about." FWCC spokesmen dismissed Hicks's sighting, still insisting that the ivory-bill is extinct in Florida, but Professor Jerome Jackson of Florida Gulf Coast University, author of *In Search of the Ivory-Billed Woodpecker* (2004), disagrees. In Jackson's view, Collier County "is the most promising place for ivory-bills. There's a possibility because so much of the Big Cypress [Swamp] is protected. There have been at least three sightings of the ivory-bills in Collier County that we simply cannot dismiss."[11]

"Extinct" Rodents

Moving from birds to mammals, we encounter the case of the silver rice rat (*Oryzomys argentatus* or *O. palustris natator*), a ten-inch rodent with silver-gray fur on its back, once found in salt marshes on nine of the Florida Keys. Researchers D. Bruce Barbour and Stephen Humphrey declared the species extinct in 1979, based on their fieldwork in its known habitat. One year later, Rhode Island mammalogist James Lazell Jr. captured a live specimen, while Numi Goodyear found silver rice rats alive and well on eight separate islands. Lazell concluded that the rats are "far from extinct, but finding specimens depends on the skill of the searcher." Lazell notes in passing that Barbour and Humphrey issued a similar verdict of extinction for the pallid beach mouse (*Peromyscus polionotus decoloratus*) and concludes that while that species "may well be extinct . . . a specious method was used to argue for extinction." The risk, as Lazell rightly notes, lies in the realm of environmental politics, because "once a species' 'extinction' is published in the refereed literature, most conservation organizations lose interest in preserving its habitat."[12]

"Specs"

On the afternoon of March 11, 1959, Bob Wall, a skin diver, was swimming off Miami Beach at a depth of thirty-five feet when he spotted a large underwater cave and went to investigate. Inside, he saw a bizarre and frightening creature whose cylindrical body, roughly five feet six inches long, was mounted on eight spiny legs, standing approximately three feet off the cave's rocky floor. The animal's pointed head sprouted twin stalks, each supporting an apparent brown-spotted eye the size of a silver dollar, trained directly on Wall. As the creature moved toward him, Wall beat a hasty retreat. He reported his sighting to the press, which dubbed the animal "Specs," but when five divers from Miami Seaquarium returned to capture Specs on March 12, no trace of it remained.[13]

Three possible explanations for Wall's sighting have thus far been advanced. The first, a deliberate hoax, seems unlikely based on Wall's reputation and apparent desire to continue his employment as a guide for the glass-bottomed tourist boat *Comrade II*. The second, favored by critics, is a simple case of mistaken identity, and cryptozoologist Karl Shuker suggests that Wall may have been spooked by a large spiny lobster (*Panulirus argus*). Arguments against this solution include the fact that spiny lobsters rarely reach two feet in length, and that Wall—an experienced diver—staunchly denied that Specs was a lobster, crab, or octopus. As noted by George Eberhart, the only known crustacean that approaches five feet in length is the Japanese spider crab (*Macrocheira kaempferi*), found only off southeastern Japan.[14]

A third, rather startling suggestion, aired by cryptozoologist Mark Hall, involves the possible survival of prehistoric eurypterids, commonly known as sea scorpions. Based on the fossil record, eurypterids reached the peak of their evolutionary development in the late Silurian period (400 million years ago) and lapsed into extinction near the end of the Permian period (about 155 million

Cryptozoologist Mark Hall suggests that "Specs" was a relict sea scorpion, presumed extinct for millions of years. (From author's collection.)

years later). Hall suggests that relict sea scorpions or their evolved descendants may account not only for Specs, but also for similar creatures reported by witnesses from Greenland to the South Pacific, and from various landlocked American states. Shuker demurs from that one-size-fits-all solution, while conceding that Specs, at least, might represent some kind of relict eurypterid.[15]

When Is Extinction the End?

It is unquestionably true, as noted by critics, that some cryptozoology "buffs" accept any wild theory advanced to explain sightings of unknown or unexpected animals. Likewise, it is certain that some "experts" have pronounced species extinct without sufficient research and have later been compelled to eat their words. From the coelacanth to the ivory-billed woodpecker, dozens of "extinct" creatures have resurfaced over time, proving reports of their demise to be premature.

How many more "living fossils"—if any—remain to be found in Florida or its surrounding waters? That question can only be answered with time and exhaustive research, but our next chapter suggests that some of those elusive cryptids may be very large indeed.

Leviathans

Throughout history, mariners have reported encounters with large marine creatures of unknown species, commonly lumped together under the name of "sea serpents." Early maps were decorated with fantastic sketches of aquatic dragons, imprinted with the warning: "Here be monsters." Many of the beasts described were neither serpentine nor reptilian in form, but the early name endures, and reports continue to the present day. While some sea monsters have been scientifically identified—including the Norse kraken, today recognized as the giant squid (*Architeuthis dux*)—others remain elusive, fueling speculation and debate.[1]

Despite the absence of type specimens, various cryptozoologists have ventured to classify marine cryptids based on anecdotal evidence. In 1968, Bernard Heuvelmans reviewed 587 sightings dating from 1622, dismissed 238 as hoaxes or "vague and therefore doubtful," and used the remainder to propose nine distinct species of large unknown creatures. Eight years later, Gary Mangiacopra simplified the list to four species, based on sixty-four reports from the nineteenth century. In 2003, Loren Coleman and Patrick Hughye identified ten marine cryptids, including a giant shark and giant octopus (considered separately in the next chapter).[2] Predictably,

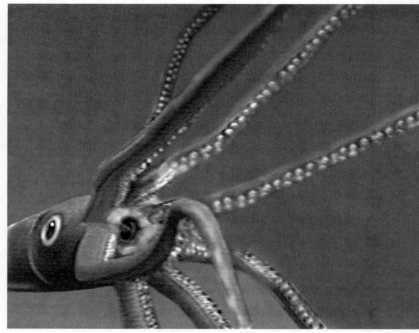

The giant squid inspired early legends of the monstrous Norse kraken. (Copyright William Rebsamen.)

such efforts produce controversy within the cryptozoological community, while inviting outright derision from skeptics.

Florida, despite its extensive maritime history, was a relative "late bloomer" where marine cryptids are concerned. The first case on record dates from 1849, and while Florida's waters have produced only seven cases to date—one involving a giant shark—they include one mysterious stranding and a unique (some say incredible) report of sea serpent predation on humans.

The *Lucy and Nancy* Creature

Florida's first known sea serpent encounter was reported in the *Boston Atlas* of February 18, 1849. According to that item, passengers aboard the schooner *Lucy and Nancy* sighted a serpentine creature some ninety feet long, with a dirty-brown back seven feet across at its widest point, swimming in the Atlantic near Cumberland Island, at the mouth of the St. Johns River. Captain Adams, apparently aboard the vessel, described the beast: "It lifted its head, which was that of a snake, several times out of the water, seemingly taking a survey of the vessel, and at such times displayed the largest portion of its body, and a pair of frightful fins or claws, several feet in length."[3]

Heuvelmans treated the sighting as authentic, but he could not decide on the creature's identity. Within his hypothetical taxonomy, he finally decided that it might represent either a mammalian "long-necked" species (presumed to be a pinniped such as a seal or walrus) or a huge "super-eel."[4]

Reports of huge "sea serpents" persist from ancient times to the present day, from all parts of the globe. (Copyright William Rebsamen.)

The New River Inlet Carcass

Large sea beasts wash ashore from time to time, and while some are easily identified, others remain unclassified. Decomposition often renders visual identification problematic, and DNA analysis has only been available since the 1980s, leaving carcasses retrieved before that time subject to speculation. One of America's most remarkable "globsters" appeared on a Florida beach in 1885, and it remains a topic of discussion to the present day.

J. B. Holder, writing for *Century* magazine seven years after the fact, reported that the creature was discovered in the spring of 1885 by Reverend George Gordon of Milwaukee, president of the American Humane Association, while his ship lay at anchor in New River Inlet (near Ft. Pierce, in St. Lucie County). When time came for the vessel to depart,

> the flukes of the anchor became foul with what proved to be a carcass of considerable length. Mr. Gordon quickly observed that it was a vertebrate, and at first thought it was probably a cetacean. But, on examination, it was seen to have features more suggestive of saurians. Its total length was forty-two feet. Its girth was six feet. The head was absent; two flippers, or fore-limbs, were noticed, and a somewhat slender neck . . . six feet in length. The carcass was in a state of decomposition; the abdomen was open, and the intestines protruded.[5]

Gordon had the rotting carcass hauled ashore and "took all possible precautions to preserve the bones until they could be removed," but a surprise hurricane intervened and swept the carcass back to sea. Florida's only hurricane of 1885 struck on August 23–24 (which hardly qualifies as "spring"), but no further details of the incident are presently available.[6]

An eyewitness sketch of the carcass found at New River Inlet in 1885. (From author's collection.)

Basking sharks (*Cetorhinus maximus*) may reach a length of forty feet, and after death their bodies often decompose in such a manner that they may present the likeness of a long-necked beast resembling a prehistoric plesiosaurus. Heuvelmans supposed that Florida's warm waters made the presence of a basking shark unlikely—a mistake on his part, though *C. maximus* apparently evacuates the Florida coast for cooler New England waters in summer—but he finally concluded that the carcass might belong to a whale shark (*Rhincodon typus*) or some other large shark of indeterminate species.[7] Without DNA testing, no more precise diagnosis is possible.

Panic at Pablo Beach

Florida's next sea monster sighting allegedly occurred at Jacksonville's Pablo Beach sometime in 1891. No further details are available, although the incident—if, in fact, it ever occurred—is memorialized in an anonymous painting, wherein four frightened swimmers bolt from the surf, gaping in terror at a dragonlike creature rising offshore, complete with forked tongue, spikes atop its head, and a serrated fin along its back. Bernard Heuvelmans included the sight-

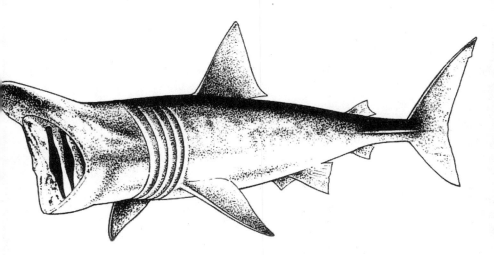

Many "sea monster" carcasses are actually decomposed basking sharks. (Dover Publications.)

No evidence supports the appearance of a sea monster at Pablo Beach, depicted in this painting from 1891. (From author's collection.)

ing in his 1968 database and reproduced the painting with a caption reading "Excitement at Pablo Beach," but he offered no further details. Ultimately Heuvelmans tagged the case with a question mark, thus ranking it among those "incomprehensible or very doubtful cases where it is impossible to tell whether they are hoaxes, mistakes or rare if not unique sightings of an animal not in my nine categories."[8] No better judgment is possible at this remove, but it seems remarkable that such an incident, complete with multiple witnesses, has otherwise escaped inclusion in the cryptozoological literature. Likewise, correspondence with local newspapers and libraries in 2005 failed to unearth any records of the case. The real surprise is that Heuvelmans did not classify the Pablo Beach incident as an outright hoax.

The *Craigsmere* Beast

In July 1920, while sailing along the Florida coast from Miami to Fort Lauderdale, seamen aboard the merchant vessel *Craigsmere* saw a large animal swimming in tandem with their vessel. Witness Charles Blackford III later described the incident to author-naturalist Ivan Sanderson: "The captain, mate on watch, helmsman and some others of the crew saw it. As I remember it they say it was long, with dorsal fins somewhat like a porpoise only several in number with its head some distance ahead of the body and partly submerged."[9]

Analyzing that report a half-century later, Bernard Heuvelmans assumed that the fins were lateral, rather than dorsal as described, thus making the creature a specimen of his hypothetical "many-finned" sea serpent.[10]

St. Andrews Bay

Nearly a quarter-century elapsed before the next report of a cryptid observed in Florida's coastal waters, in late March 1943. Author Thomas Helm and his wife were yachting on St. Andrews Bay, south of Panama City, when a strange creature rose from the depths and swam toward their boat, displaying "a head about the size of a basketball on a neck which reached nearly four feet out of the water." The head and neck were covered with wet, glistening fur. "My first thought," Helm recalled, "was that we were seeing some kind of giant otter or seal, but I was immediately impressed by the fact that this was not the face of an otter or seal."[11] He continued:

The head of this creature, with the exception that there was no evidence of ears, was that of a monstrous cat. The face was fur covered and the eyes were set in the front of the head. The color of the wet fur was uniformly a rich chocolate brown. The well-defined eyes were about the size of a silver dollar and were glistening black. There was evidence of a flattened black nose and just below . . . was a mustache of stiff black hairs with a downward curve on each side.[12]

While Helm initially suspected that the creature was a pinniped, he finally rejected that theory on the grounds that no relative of the seals has such a long neck (which is true) or such a large head (which is false, in the case of the elephant seal). A third grounds for rejection was the supposed extinction of seals in the Gulf of Mexico since the Caribbean monk seal (*Monarchus tropicalis*) was exterminated. Still, monk seals were not declared extinct until 1950, and persistent sightings continued through the 1990s. Heuvelmans accepted Helm's sighting as legitimate and classified the creature as a specimen of his hypothetical "merhorse," a long-necked mammal with large eyes and a flowing mane.[13]

Edward McCleary's Tale

The most startling "sea serpent" story from Florida waters—or, arguably, from anywhere else—is that told by Edward Brian McCleary, concerning the alleged events of March 24, 1962. On that date, at age sixteen, McCleary and four male companions reportedly set off from Pensacola on a raft to dive upon the *Massachusetts,* a sunken ship offshore. A storm caught them at sea and pulled them farther from the coastline than expected, leaving them adrift and lost in fog. After an hour's aimless drifting, they began to hear "strange noises, rather like the splashing of a porpoise or other large fish [*sic*]," accompanied by "a sickening odor like that of dead fish." As the splashing sounds moved closer, the five friends also heard "a loud hissing sound," then saw "what looked like a pole, about ten feet high, sticking straight up out of the water. On top was a bulb-like structure." That curious object "bent in the middle" and submerged, then surfaced once more, repeating the procedure as it drew ever closer.[14]

Panic ensued. McCleary later explained that the boys were "too terrified to think clearly" as they donned swim fins and abandoned the raft. Separated from his friends in the fog, McCleary soon heard them screaming "one by one." Finally, he "got a closer look at the thing just as my last friend went under." Its neck was twelve feet long, brownish green in color, and "smooth looking," surmounted by a head resembling a sea turtle's "except more elongated, with teeth." Its eyes, McCleary said, were "green with oval pupils." McCleary somehow made it to the sunken ship that had been his original target, climbing aboard "the top part . . . which protruded from

Artist's depiction of an alleged sea monster attack off Pensacola in 1962, described by "survivor" Edward McCleary. (Copyright William Rebsamen.)

the water," and clung there until morning, when he "swam to shore and was found by the rescue unit."[15]

McCleary's account is the only modern claim of "sea serpent" predation on humans, and it naturally raises some questions. First among them is the lack of coverage by local newspapers, which seems remarkable for a quadruple drowning, even in the absence of a monster. While multiple deaths of teenagers normally capture headlines, McCleary's adventure seemingly went unnoticed until 1965, when he published a first-person account in *Fate Magazine,* a popular journal devoted to unexplained phenomena. One Internet source claims the story was "published in a local Pensacola newspaper," but no further details were provided, and queries to the webmaster proved fruitless.[16] Likewise, queries to the Pensacola Police Department, the Escambia County Sheriff's Department, the U.S. Coast Guard, the *Gulf Herald,* and the *Pensacola News Journal* proved fruitless.

Assuming for a moment that some version of the tragedy occurred in fact, what happened to McCleary's friends? Unfortunately, published sources are confused and contradictory. McCleary's 1965 account and a subsequent, more detailed version sent to author Tim Dinsdale, include no reference to the recovery of bodies. One Internet source claims (without supporting documentation) that "[o]ne boy apparently panicked and drowned. The other three apparently were eaten." A second Web source, likewise unburdened by evidence, claims that three of McCleary's friends vanished, "with only one later discovered by rescue units." No source provides their names or any other details to facilitate investigation of the case. Authors William Gibbons and Kent Hovind assert that Coast Guard searchers found one of the boys, "who apparently drowned." Dr. Heuvelmans, writing three years after the supposed events, left his readers to decide if "it [is] literally true, a complete hoax, or is there some other explanation?"[17]

One curious aspect of the McCleary tale is the manner in which Christian fundamentalists have seized upon it to support their case for "young Earth" creationism. In their view, reports of marine cryptids (or alleged living dinosaurs in Third World jungles) demonstrate that Earth is no more than six thousand years old. Kent "Dr. Dino" Hovind, a controversial proponent of that theory, has published the name of a Florida resident, alleged to be the stepmother of "one of the boys that was eaten" in March 1962.[18] As research for the work in hand, I wrote to the address provided by Hovind and received no answer.

Myakka River

The year 1962 also produced reports of another "sea monster," sighted by witnesses around Englewood, six hundred miles to the southeast in Sarasota County. There, according to *Englewood Sun* reporter Diana Harris, who researched the incident for an article published in 2006, several unnamed individuals reported sightings of a thirty-foot serpentine creature swimming "in or near the Myakka River." At the time, a local herpetologist suggested that the beast might be an anaconda, and he offered to capture it "provided we have five or six husky men to hold the body," but volunteers failed to materialize, and the animal remains unidentified today. Harris provided no specific dates for those events but noted that a rare oarfish (*Regalecus glesne* Ascanius) that beached at nearby Manasota Key before year's end "was immediately labeled a sea monster."[19]

In response to personal inquiries for this volume, Harris was unable to produce specific sources for her article of January 14, 2006, but she asserted that both stories were reported in the *Englewood Herald* sometime during 1962. My inquiries to other local newspapers and libraries proved fruitless, but an oarfish might explain the sightings (if, in fact, they occurred). Oarfish twenty-six feet long have been confirmed, and lengths of up to fifty-five feet have been alleged by some witnesses. Strandings of oarfish on Florida's coast are uncommon, but two specimens have surfaced so far in the twenty-first century. A specimen stranded in March 2002, on Anna Maria Island, south of Tampa Bay, measured thirteen feet long, while an immature specimen beached on Marco's Sand Dollar Island, two years later, measured eight feet, six inches.[20]

A Giant Shark

Our last report of a marine cryptid from Florida waters involves a "giant" shark of unknown species—or, perhaps, *another* giant shark, if we assume that the New River Inlet carcass belonged to a selachian (cartilaginous fish). Thomas Helm, the same writer who had described his encounter with the St. Andrews Bay creature in 1943, also described his encounter with a large shark of unknown species, seen on a fishing excursion from St. Andrews in the late 1940s.

Helm was working aboard a sixty-foot commercial fishing boat when the propeller shaft was fouled with baling wire. A crewman dived to clear the shaft, but he was soon recalled aboard when a huge shark appeared, circling the boat. One sailor opined that the fish was "nearbout as long as this here boat," but Helm made a more precise measurement when the shark swam slowly underneath the vessel. Its pectoral fins protruded on either side of the trawler, and "once when his huge tail was even with the stern his head was just below the midship booms! By actual measurement the shark was not an inch less than thirty feet!" As detailed by Helm, "The color on his upper parts was dark. It may have been black, dark brown or dark blue, and in general conformation he most closely resembled the white shark."[21]

Great white sharks (*Carcharodon carcharias*) are the stuff of mariners' legends and Hollywood horror films, solitary predators ranked as the largest carnivorous fish in the world—but how large do they grow? Sensational claims of white sharks forty-three feet long have been published, sans documentation, but the record official claim—at 36.5 feet, listed in an 1870 catalog of the British Museum of Natural History—proved to be a misprint and actually referred to a specimen 16.5 feet long. A nineteen-foot specimen is documented from Chilean waters, and a white shark twenty-three feet long was allegedly caught off Kangaroo Island, South Australia, in May 1987, but only one of its pectoral fins was preserved as evidence. While other accounts describe specimens ranging from twenty to thirty feet long, Richard Ellis concludes from exhaustive archival research that "the largest white sharks accurately measured range between 19 and 21 feet."[22] Thus, if Helm's thirty-foot specimen was a great white, it qualifies as a cryptid of sorts in its own right.

The giant whale shark bears no resemblance to the fish seen by Thomas Helm off St. Andrews in the late 1940s. (Dover Publications.)

Some cryptozoologists believe that specimens of the whale-sized *Carcharodon megalodon* may still survive. (Copyright William Rebsamen.)

What else may it have been? The world's largest fish is the whale shark, at fifty feet, but no fisherman worth his salt could mistake that speckled plankton-feeder for a great white. The basking shark is a somewhat more likely pretender, but the species is unknown on Florida's Gulf Coast. A third possibility, however remote, lies in the theoretical survival of *Carcharodon megalodon*, a whale-sized ancestor of the great white shark, whose six-inch fossil teeth suggest it had a total length between sixty and eighty feet. Although widely presumed extinct since the late Tertiary period, some fifty million years ago, *C. megalodon* may have survived much later. Indeed, analysis performed in 1959 on two teeth dredged from the Atlantic during 1875 revealed that one specimen was twenty-four thousand years old, while the other was a mere eleven thousand years old. Sightings of truly giant "white sharks" from the Pacific and Indian Oceans, recorded between 1918 and 1954, raise the intriguing possibility that *C. megalodon* may still prowl modern seas.[23]

Fish Stories or Fact?

Unlike some other regions—British Columbia, New England, Vietnam's Along Bay—Florida has no tradition of persistent or "dependable" sea monsters. Six incidents spanning 113 years hardly establishes the state's coastline as a happy hunting ground for cryptozoologists, but even that meager sampling may be analyzed.

Of Florida's seven sightings, two—at Pablo Peach and Pensacola—must be shelved until such time as further information is available. Both may be hoaxes, but the evidence on hand (or lack of same) permits no final judgment. Of the five cases remaining, two—the New River Inlet carcass and Thomas Helm's great shark—involve large selachians of indeterminate species. The last three sightings, in 1849, 1920, and 1943, are more problematic. Dr. Heuvelmans concluded that all three creatures were mammals, albeit of different species, though he wavered on the first, suggesting that it also may have been a "super-eel."[24] Again, without type specimens or decent photographs, the question must remain forever unanswered.

Our next case, also from the sea, presents a rather different problem. Investigators have both photographs and samples of the creature's flesh to study, but despite a century of argument, they still cannot agree on what it was.

4

Octopus giganteus

Most cryptid sightings are exactly that—sightings. Eyewitnesses report their brief encounters with some creature they cannot identify, while others who were nowhere near the scene dissect, explain, and often ridicule their stories. Some encounters produce blurry photographs, a tuft of hair, disputed tracks, but nothing that qualifies as evidence within the rigorous view of mainstream science. Only the beast itself, alive or dead, will satisfy the calls for proof. In 1896, nature delivered one such specimen in Florida, but as this chapter demonstrates, even a cryptid in the flesh may not resolve debates concerning its identity.

Something on the Beach

On November 30, 1896, while bicycling to Matanzas Inlet on St. Augustine's Anastasia Island, Herbert Coles and Dunham Coretter discovered a large rotting carcass half-buried in sand near Crescent Beach. They hurried home to report their find, and word soon reached Dr. DeWitt Webb, founder of the St. Augustine Historical Society and Institute of Science. Webb presumed the stranded beast to be a whale but changed his mind when he observed the carcass

Workers stand beside the "globster" beached at St. Augustine in November 1896. (From author's collection.)

for himself on the first of December. Webb measured the lump of flesh, but his precise results are lost in various accounts: a letter dated December 8, 1896, describes the carcass as eighteen feet long and ten feet wide; other reports published between December 1, 1896, and 2003 variously describe it as measuring anywhere from eighteen to twenty-three feet long, seven to eighteen feet wide, and four to six feet high, with an estimated weight of five to seven tons. The animal's skin was light pink, nearly white, with a silvery sheen. Webb noted the apparent stumps of four severed arms and also found one of the arms itself, buried nearby. The creature, he concluded, must have been a giant octopus.[1]

Jacksonville's *Florida Times-Union* broke the story on December 1 with an article headlined, "Big Octopus on the Beach," and the story surfaced in the *New York Herald* one day later, curiously headlined "Last of This Sea Serpent." That article expanded the carcass to eighteen feet wide (an apparent typographical error) and added the observation that its skin "is very tough and cannot be penetrated, even with a sharp penknife."[2]

Back in St. Augustine, meanwhile, Webb continued his study of the carcass on December 5 and 7, drawing sketches and posing beside it for photographs. On December 8, Webb sent his photos and a brief description of the carcass to J. A. Allen at Harvard University's Museum of Comparative Zoology. Allen passed the information on to Professor Addison Verrill at Yale, then recognized as America's leading expert on cephalopods. Based on the information he received, Verrill initially believed the carcass to be that of a giant squid (*Architeuthis dux*).[3]

Webb's letter and photos were still in transit on December 13, 1896, when Dr. George Grant, owner of a hotel at nearby South Beach, penned a short article for *Grit* (a tabloid published from Williamsport, Pennsylvania). Grant described the St. Augustine carcass as follows:

The head is as large as an ordinary flour barrel, and has the shape of a sea lion head. The neck, if the creature may be said to have a neck, is of the same diameter as the body. The mouth is on the under side of the head and is protected by two tenacle [sic] tubes about eight inches in diameter and about 30 feet long. These tubes resemble an elephant's trunk and obviously were used to clutch in a sucker like fashion any object within their reach. Another tube or tenacle [sic] of the same dimensions stands out on top of the head. Two others, one on each side, protrude from beyond the monster's neck, and extend fully 15 feet along the body and beyond the tail. The tail, which is separated and jagged with cutting points for several feet, is flanked by two more tenacles [sic] of the same dimensions as the others and 30 feet long. The eyes are under the back of the mouth instead of over it. This specimen is so badly cut up by sharks and sawfish that only the stumps of the tentacles remain, but pieces of them were found strewn for some distance on the beach, showing that the animal had a fierce battle with its foes before it was disabled and beached by the surf.[4]

Grant proposed to build a shed around the carcass and charge admission, but Webb dissuaded him with a plea on behalf of science. Professor Verrill, meanwhile, had revised his opinion of the creature, writing to the *New York Herald* on January 3, 1897:

Dr. Webb has sent me photographs, four different pictures of the animal. They were taken on the same day he examined it. They show that the body is flattened, pear shaped, largest near the back end, which is broadly rounded and without fins. This form of the body and its proportions show that it is an eight-armed cuttlefish, or octopus, and not a ten-armed squid like the devil fish of other regions. No such gigantic octopus has been heretofore discovered.[5]

Verrill followed that brief acknowledgment with an article for the *American Journal of Science* in February 1897, wherein he estimated the creature's dimensions in life based on comparison to smaller species. Verrill calculated that the giant's tentacles may have been seventy-five to a hundred feet long, and eighteen inches thick at the base. "This species," he wrote, "is evidently distinct from all known forms, and I therefore propose to name it *Octopus giganteus*. It is possible that it may be related to *Cirroteuthis,* and in that case the two posterior stumps, looking like arms, may be the remains of lateral fins, for they seem too far back for the arms, unless pulled out of position."[6]

Verrill's change of heart was probably influenced by the findings of another St. Augustine local, John L. Wilson, who excavated sand

Another photo of the St. Augustine carcass, taken in January 1897. (From author's collection.)

A different view of the carcass, also photographed in January 1897. (From author's collection.)

around the carcass and discovered pieces of its severed tentacles. According to Wilson, "One arm was lying west of the body, twenty-three feet long; one stump of arm, west of body, about four feet; three arms lying south of the body and from appearance attached to same (although I did not dig quite to body, as it lay well down in the sand, and I was very tired), longest measured over thirty-two feet, the other arms were three to five feet shorter." Before Webb could confirm those findings, a storm swept the carcass back out to sea, then returned it to the beach (sans severed arms) some two miles from its previous location.[7]

To prevent further losses, Webb hired a team of men and horses on January 16, 1897, and dragged the carcass forty feet inland, placed it on boards, and staked it down with ropes. After further correspondence with Verrill and Professor William Dall, curator of mollusks at the Smithsonian Institution in Washington, D.C., Webb excised pieces of the animal's flesh and mailed them off to the experts.[8] Webb's letter to Dall, dated February 5, explained:

I made another excursion to the invertebrate and brought away specimens for you and Dr. Verrill of Yale. I cut two pieces of the mantle and two pieces from the body and have put them in a solution of formalin for a few days before I sent them to you. Although strange as it may seem to you, I could have packed them in salt and sent them to you at once although the creature had been lying on the beach for more than two months. And I think that both yourself and Dr. Verrill, while not doubting my measurements, have thought my account of the thickness of the muscular, or rather tenebrous husk pretty large, so I am glad to send you the specimens and I will express them packed in salt in a day or two.[9]

The specimens were still in transit when Verrill submitted a paper to the *American Journal of Science,* in which he appeared to retreat from his previous verdict on the creature, reverting to a claim that it must be giant squid. After dismissing John Wilson's report of severed arms as "erroneous and entirely misleading," Verrill concluded:

The proportions indicate that this might have been a squid-like form, and not an *Octopus.* The "breadth" is evidently that of the softened and collapsed body, and would represent an actual maximum diameter in life of at least 7 feet and a probable weight of 4 or 5 tons for the body and head. These dimensions are decidedly larger than those of the well-authenticated Newfoundland specimens. It is perhaps a species of *Architeuthis.*[10]

Addison Verrill drew this sketch to accompany his first article on the giant octopus in February 1897. (From author's collection.)

A second sketch drawn by Verrill in February 1897. (From author's collection.)

On February 14, 1897, still without specimens in hand, Verrill changed his mind again. This time, writing for the *New York Herald*, he described what was clearly a huge octopus:

> The living weight of the creature was about eighteen or twenty tons. When living, it must have had enormous arms, each one a hundred feet or more in length, each as thick as the mast of a large vessel, and armed with hundreds of saucer-shaped suckers, the largest of which would have been at least a foot in diameter. . . . Its eyes would have been more than a foot in diameter. It would have carried ten or twelve gallons of ink in the ink bag. It could swim rapidly, without doubt, but its usual habit would be to crawl slowly over the bottom in deep water in pursuit of prey. . . . We must reflect that wherever this creature had its home, there must be living hundreds or even thousands of others of its kind, probably of equal size, otherwise its race could not be kept up.[11]

Verrill finally received Webb's specimens on February 23, 1897, and his opinion dramatically changed once again. He subsequently penned letters of retraction, published in the *American Journal of Science* on March 5 and in the *New York Herald* two days later. Withdrawing his proposed Latin name for the beast, Verrill wrote, "The supposition that it was an *Octopus* was partly based upon its baglike form and partly upon the statements made to me that the stumps of large arms were attached to it at first. This last statement was certainly untrue." In fact, he claimed, "[W]hen it was excavated and moved, . . . nothing that can be called stumps of arms, or any other appendages were present. Folds of the integument and mutilated and partly detached portions may have been mistaken for such structures."[12]

As for the samples in hand, Verrill wrote, "These masses are from 3 to 10 inches thick, and instead of being muscular, as had been thought, they have a structure similar to the hard, elastic variety of blubber-like integument found on the head of certain cetaceans, such as the sperm whale. Although such an integument might, perhaps, be supposed compatible with the structure of some unknown fish or reptile, it is certain that it is more like the integument found upon the upper head of a sperm whale than anything else I know." That said, Verrill concluded that it must indeed be part of a whale, although "what part of any cetacean it might have been is still an unsolved puzzle."[13]

On March 13, 1897, the *St. Augustine Tatler* lampooned Verrill's verdict in an editorial:

> Professor Verrill of Yale University, who recently decided that the curious something, supposed to be an octopus, was one, basing his decision on descriptions sent, has now concluded, after examining a piece of it, that it could not possibly be an octopus, and he cannot decide what it is. One theory advanced is that it may be a portion of some other inhabitant of the sea, long since extinct, that has been fast in an iceberg for centuries, and recently washed ashore here. Another theory is that it is a portion of a deep-sea monster that on coming too near the surface was attacked by a shark, who found it too tough for breakfast. One thing is now determined, and that is, if we do not know what it is, we know what it is not.[14]

Webb wrote once again to William Dall on March 17, disputing Verrill's latest claims. "As you already know," he wrote, "Prof. Verrill now says our strange creature cannot be a cephalopod and that he cannot say to what animal it belongs. I do not see how it can be any part of a cetacean as Prof. V. says you suggest. It is simply a great big bag and I do not see how it could be any part of a whale. Now that I have had it brought 6 miles up the beach it is out of the way of the tide and the drifting sand and will have a chance to cure or dry up somewhat. If it were not for the mass of the viscera which was so difficult to remove that we left it there would be but little odor. As it is there is no great amount." Regrettably, no answering letter from Dall has survived, nor was his judgment of the tissue samples anywhere recorded.[15]

Professor Verrill defended his latest verdict in *Science* on March 19, resorting to arguments that author Richard Ellis terms "bizarre." On that occasion, Verrill wrote: "The structure of the integument is more like that of the upper part of the head of a sperm whale than any other known to me, and as the obvious use is the same, it is most probable that the whole mass represents the upper part of the head of such a whale, detached from the skull and jaw. It is evident, however, from the figures, that the shape is decidedly unlike the head of an ordinary sperm whale, for the latter is oblong, truncated and rather narrow in front, like the prow of a vessel with an angle at the upper front end, near which a single blow hole is situated." To buttress his argument, Verrill ventured to "imagine a sperm whale with an abnormally large nose, due to disease or old age," finally concluding that "it seems hardly probable that another allied whale, with a big nose, remains to be discovered." Dr. Frederic Lucas, the Smithsonian's curator of comparative anatomy, supported Verrill with a letter to the same issue of *Science*, writing: "The substance looks like blubber, and smells like blubber, and it *is* blubber, nothing more nor less."[16]

Verrill continued to defend his judgment over the next two months. In the April 1897 issue of *American Naturalist* he wrote, "[M]y present opinion, that it came from the head of a creature like a sperm whale in structure, is the only one that seems plausible from the facts now ascertained." His last word on the subject, published in the May 1897 *American Journal of Science*, bore the dismissive title "The Supposed Great Octopus of Florida: Certainly Not a Cephalopod." From London that same month, the editors of *Natu-*

ral Science chided Verrill: "The moral of this is that one should not attempt to describe specimens on the coast of Florida, while sitting in one's study in Connecticut."[17]

Debate Resumed

The matter rested there for sixty years, while much important evidence was lost. Tireless researcher Gary Mangiacopra subsequently learned that Verrill's samples of the St. Augustine creature vanished sometime between 1911 (when Yale's old museum was demolished) and 1926 (when a new one was completed). Three decades after that, in 1957, an old newspaper clipping on the case found its way to Dr. Forrest Wood, a curator at Florida's Marineland. Intrigued, Wood undertook his own investigation and discovered that the specimens Webb sent to Dall in 1896 were still intact at the Smithsonian. Wood alerted a colleague, cellular biologist Joseph Gennaro at the University of Florida, and Gennaro flew to Washington. At the museum, he found "half a dozen large white masses of tough fibrous material, each about as large as a good-sized roast," preserved in formalin and alcohol.[18]

Although the number of samples on hand tripled that reportedly sent to Dall by Webb in 1896, Gennaro and company somehow confirmed their identity. Upon receiving permission to excise two pieces for study, Gennaro dulled four scalpel blades in the process of securing the bits desired. The tissue's toughness was anomalous for blubber, which confirmed the observations in a letter discovered by Wood, sent by Dr. Webb to Verrill sixty years before. On that occasion, Webb had written, "The hood is so tough that when it is exposed to the air, an axe makes very little impression on it." Verrill, at the time, agreed that the samples were "so tough that it is hard to cut them, even with a razor, and yet they are somewhat flexible and elastic." Gennaro examined the Florida samples under a polarizing microscope, comparing them to known samples from octopus and squid, finally pronouncing their cross-hatched connective tissue "similar to, if not identical with, that in my octopus sample." In Gennaro's words, "The evidence appears unmistakable that the St.

Augustine sea monster was in fact an octopus, but the implications are fantastic."[19]

Wood and Gennaro published their findings in *Natural History* (March 1971). Four years later, Gary Mangiacopra summarized the convoluted tale in print and christened the great beast *Octopus giganteus* Verrill. Roy Mackal devoted a chapter to the case in his first book on cryptozoology, *Searching for Hidden Animals* (1980), including side-by-side micrographs of tissue from an octopus, a squid, and the St. Augustine creature. Six years later, in the peer-reviewed journal *Cryptozoology*, Mackal published results from a biochemical study of the Smithsonian samples. That survey compared amino acid composition of the Florida samples with known tissue from a dolphin, a beluga whale, a giant squid, and two species of contemporary octopus. Comparisons were also made to the amino acid levels found in bone and collagen extracted from a cow and human being. Mackal concluded that the Florida carcass "was essentially a huge mass of collagenous protein" and "[c]ertainly . . . was not blubber." His findings pointed to "a gigantic cephalopod, probably an octopus, not referable to any known species."[20]

The question thus appeared to be resolved, once and for all. As late as 1994, author Richard Ellis—ever ready to debunk "sea monsters"—dismissed attempts to brand the St. Augustine carcass as portions of a whale. His flat conclusion: "It was a giant octopus." The ink was barely dry on that report when scientists from the University of Maryland (College Park) and the Indianapolis Faculty of Medicine issued a contrary finding. Their study of the Smithsonian tissue, published in the *Biological Bulletin* (April 1995), concluded that the tested sample was in fact skin collagen from a cetacean's blubber. French cryptozoologist Michel Raynal fired back with a critique of that study, listing various methodological problems, and dismissed its conclusion as "complete nonsense."[21]

What If?

The ongoing debate over Florida's "globster" does not exist in a vacuum. In fact, giant octopus sightings have been recorded from the

Reports of giant cephalopods persist from the Caribbean in modern times. (Copyright William Rebsamen.)

Caribbean region throughout history, supporting the hypothesis of Roy Mackal and others that a deceased specimen might drift northward with the Florida Current, washing ashore anywhere from Fort Pierce to North Carolina's Long Bay.[22]

In 1941, while sailing aboard the USS *Chicopee* Ao-41 between Fort Lauderdale and St. Augustine, coxswain John Martin spied some object resembling a huge knot of kelp on the surface nearby. Closer observation left him in "no doubt" that the object was alive—a massive octopus, in fact, some thirty feet across, with arms of equal length "coiled but moving slowly." Martin estimated that each tentacle measured more than three feet in circumference.[23]

In 1956, a full year before he first read of St. Augustine's monster, Forrest Wood encountered tales of giant cephalopods in the Bahamas. A native guide regaled Wood with descriptions of "giant scuttles" with tentacles seventy-five feet long, and the commissioner of Andros Island recalled a boyhood encounter with a "very large" octopus that snagged his father's fishing line at a depth of some six hundred feet. Native traditions on Andros describe huge cephalopods known as "Lusca," or "Him of the Hands," that menace divers in the region's deep "blue holes." Bruce Wright, director of New Brunswick's Northeastern Wildlife Station, detailed the Lusca's history in 1967 but opined that they were giant squids. Bernard Heuvelmans and Michel Raynal subsequently traced reports of giant Caribbean cephalopods back to 1500, when Pietro Martire (biographer of Christopher Columbus) reported one such creature snatching a hapless Spaniard from an island beach.[24]

More recently, in 1984, Bermudan fisherman John Ingham complained that a giant octopus had wreaked havoc with his crab and shrimp traps. On several occasions in August and September, Ingham lost traps while hauling them up from depths of fifteen hundred to three thousand feet. In each case, his line (guaranteed up to forty-five hundred pounds) snapped under a "tremendous weight." On September 16, 1984, some unseen creature towed Ingham's fifty-foot boat for close to half an hour, while Ingham's chromoscope (sonar) fish-finder etched images of "a pyramid shape approximately 50 feet high." Bennie Rohr, a marine biologist then employed by the U.S. National Marine Fisheries Service at Pascagoula, Mississippi, opined that Ingham's deep-sea nemesis was a giant octopus. Ingham allegedly confirmed it a year later, when he brought one of the monsters to the surface, still attached to one of his traps. He tried to hook it but succeeded only in procuring a fifty-pound lump of ragged tissue before the wounded beast submerged. Smithsonian scientists were unable to identify the sample from photographs, and Ingham apparently withheld the tissue itself from study.[25]

In August 1999, researcher James Plaskett launched his own

search for a giant Bahamian octopus, funded by Demon Internet founder Cliff Stanford. Plaskett's team submerged cameras at various points throughout John Ingham's old fishing grounds, baited with fish to attract predators, but the largest creature caught on film was a fifteen-foot shark. Ingham could not be reached for comment on the theory that a shark that size might tow his boat or snap his heavy-duty fishing lines.[26]

What Next?

The largest octopus recognized by science, *Enteroctopus dolfeini,* is a Pacific species known to exceed one hundred pounds, with a radial spread of twenty feet. The record specimen, caught off the British Columbian coast in 1967, measured twenty-three feet at full spread and tipped the scales at 156 pounds. A smaller subspecies, *E. megalocyathus,* inhabits the eastern South Pacific and South Atlantic, including Argentinean waters, but is presently unknown in the Caribbean.[27] Since the prospect of a freakish *E. dolfeini* specimen—ten times the record size and half a world beyond its normal range—seems ludicrous, what are the other possibilities?

The spermaceti tank of a sperm whale (*Physeter macrocephalus*) may indeed explain the St. Augustine carcass, though the hypothetical diseased whale with "a big nose" remains a creature of Professor Verrill's imagination. Such spermaceti tanks are rich in collagen, possess a baglike shape, and typically weigh several tons. It is regrettable that Mackal's tests in 1986 employed tissue from a beluga whale (*Delphinapterus leucas*) rather than *P. macrocephalus,* but the fact remains that amino acid levels in the St. Augustine samples were strikingly different from those found in either whale or dolphin tissue.[28]

A second proposed explanation—that the St. Augustine carcass was a beached sunfish (*Mola mola*)—may be quickly dismissed. Despite its peculiar shape, scaleless skin, and relatively large size (up to eleven feet and forty-four hundred pounds), the sunfish in fact bears no credible resemblance to the mysterious specimen that washed up. The largest specimen on record is too small to compete with St. Augustine's giant, while Webb and the other observers could hardly have missed its bony skeleton.[29]

We are left, finally, with the choice between a mangled whale and a huge unknown species of cephalopod. Michel Raynal proposed a new Latin name, *Otoctopus giganteus* ("giant eared-octopus"), to explain the anomalous rear-end flaps that puzzled so many observers. Bernard Heuvelmans suggested a giant form of ciliated octopus (*Cirroteuthis*), although the largest specimen on record measured eight feet long while swimming with its tentacles extended. Neither species has yet been brought to light and formally classified.[30]

George Eberhart observes that an amino-acid sequence analysis or collagen electrophoresis test might resolve the cetacean-cephalopod argument once and for all, but he also warns that the Florida samples may now be too degraded and contaminated for definitive testing.[31] In any case, no further efforts have been made within the past decade to solve the enduring riddle of *Octopus giganteus* Verrill.

Freshwater Phantoms

Around the world, throughout recorded history, freshwater cryptid sightings have been logged from every continent except Antarctica. Loch Ness and Lake Champlain are two of the most famous "monster" lakes, but hundreds more boast histories of sightings, some of which continue to the present day. In the United States alone, researchers list 222 lakes and rivers as alleged cryptid habitats. Research on the phenomenon is so widespread that it now constitutes a subdiscipline of cryptozoology, dubbed "dracontology."[1]

That said, it must be noted that a major problem presently exists where research on freshwater cryptids is concerned. Specifically, some authors have become enamored of producing lists that catalog supposed "monster" lakes and rivers, subdivided by continents, countries, states, and provinces, presumed to be definitive but providing no information on the lakes or their alleged cryptic inhabitants. Because such lists feed on one another, both in print and on the Internet, republished over decades, their authoritative appearance is in fact misleading. As a case in point, three lists published by respected authors Loren Coleman and John Kirk between 1983 and 2001 include Lake La Metrie, Wyoming, as a site of cryptid encounters. In fact, no such lake exists, although a fictional story

Neither Lake La Metrie nor its monster, shown in this illustration from 1899, actually exists. (From author's collection.)

published in 1899, "The Monster of Lake La Metrie," describes it in melodramatic detail.[2]

Listing of "monster" lakes apparently began in 1980, with a short roster in Roy Mackal's *Searching for Hidden Animals*. One year later, British authors Janet Bord and Colin Bord offered a global list of 265 lakes and rivers in *Alien Animals*. Loren Coleman listed North American freshwater sites in both editions of *Mysterious America* (1983, 2001). The Bords amplified their worldwide list in 1989, for *Unexplained Mysteries of the 20th Century*. Canadian author Betty Garner published a list of North American freshwater sites in *Monster! Monster!* (1995), and fellow countryman John Kirk furnished another global list three years later, in his book *In the Domain of the Lake Monsters*. George Eberhart's *Mysterious Creatures* listed 884 "monster-infested bodies of water" in 2002, while Loren Coleman and Patrick Huyghe's *Field Guide to Lake Monsters, Sea Serpents, and Other Mystery Denizens of the Deep* (2003) offers "nearly 1,000" freshwater locations. Several Web sites also reproduce the lists published in volumes here named, with or without credit to the original compilers.[3]

All of the authors named above are known for the high quality of their archival research, field investigations, and (in general) the accuracy of their published work. Unfortunately, where the lake lists are concerned, it seems that some of them uncritically accept the published work of others and thereby unwittingly perpetuate certain mistakes. As we shall see, even where lakes are accurately named and located, most of the lists provide no dates or other details for alleged cryptid sightings. Two of the eight freshwater cryptid sites in Florida unfortunately fall into that "twilight zone" where rumor takes the place of fact.

Lake Clinch

At least five books, published between 1983 and 2003, name Lake Clinch—near Frostproof, in Polk County—as a source of freshwater cryptid reports. Regrettably, none supplies a word of information beyond the lake's name.[4] My own inquiries to local libraries and newspapers failed to produce any leads or archival reports. It is entirely possible that Lake Clinch *has* produced some cryptid sightings in the past, or that it may figure in aboriginal mythology, but as of press time for the work in hand, no further information was available.

Lake Monroe

The same five books cited above include Lake Monroe, north of Sanford in Volusia County, on their lists of supposed cryptid habitats. Once again, as with Lake Clinch, they offer no details.[5] And once again, my own research through local libraries and newspapers produced no folktales or reported sightings to support a claim of unknown creatures in the lake. If such reports exist outside of rumor, they have failed to reach the media or surface in the standard literature of dracontology.

Goose Lake

Thankfully, more information is available concerning the supposed monster of Putnam County's Goose Lake, although it appears on none of the published lists. According to a newspaper report published on October 25, 1881, fishermen N. G. Osborne, J. Z. Scott, and Aaron Terry sighted a creature "between fifteen and twenty feet in length, and as large around as a common horse. It has a head like a dog and a tail like a catfish." Its body was covered with "long hair of a dark color." No fins or legs were seen, the beast reportedly swimming "with the motion of a fish, rather than that of a snake." The animal seemed fond of trailing lighted boats at night, until Osborne and Terry speared it, whereupon it "freed itself with a violent effort, twisting the prongs of the gig like so many straws."[6] No later accounts of the creature have surfaced.

Indian River "Sea Serpent"

Sightings of a large freshwater cryptid in the Indian River, near Titusville, began in late February 1895. The early reports were dismissed as fanciful, until a morning in March when hundreds gathered to meet an arriving steamer. At 9 a.m. the crowd spied a large dark object lying seventy-five feet offshore. Mistaking the object for wreckage, two men identified as Captain Simmonds and Fred White approached the object in a rowboat. As they neared, it raised "a wicked looking head with basilisk eyes," hissed loudly, and swam toward their boat, approaching close enough for the frightened men to see its teeth and smell its breath. Witnesses estimated the "serpent's" length at sixty feet, its girth equivalent to a barrel's at the widest point. "For about six feet along in back," one said, "there appeared to be a row of fins. The body of the reptile tapered gradually to a pointed tail." Simmonds and White reached shore unscathed, but desperate for "restoratives." The *Atlanta Constitution* reported that "[t]he appearance of the monster has demoralized tourist travel on the Indian [R]iver and the house boats of the wealthy northerners have been deserted."[7] All in vain, it seems, since the beast did not return.

The Astor Monster

Another "beast of the deep" has haunted Astor, in Lake County, for more than a century. The first reports date from 1896, when fishermen and passengers aboard a steamboat met the creature on Lake Dexter. Further sightings were logged in the 1940s and 1950s. In 1953, boaters on Lake Dexter claimed that a thirty-five-foot creature swam beside their craft, then veered toward shore, left the water, and vanished into the forest. In the late 1960s, fishing guide Buck Dillard and two of his clients encountered a beast "the size of an elephant" while trolling on the St. Johns River near Lake Dexter. Dillard says the creature *walked* along the river bottom, thus presumably eliminating possible confusion with a manatee. In 1987, two fishermen on Lake Dexter reported that a large, unseen beast tipped their boat from below, leaving a four-foot-long dent in its hull.[8]

"Pinky"

Florida's St. Johns River is sometimes called "the American Nile." It is one of the few American rivers that flow northward, meandering from Brevard County's Lake Hell 'n' Blazes through a chain of lakes and swamps before it broadens and veers eastward to meet the sea at Jacksonville, 310 miles from its headwaters. Beginning in the 1950s, Jacksonville newspapers carried reports of a large, unknown creature lurking in the St. Johns. A decade later, while bow hunting along the river, biology student Mary Lou Richardson and two companions saw an aquatic beast with a flat head and relatively short neck paddling in the water. Four other groups of tourists reported similar sightings the same afternoon, and inquiries by Ivan Sanderson revealed that the creature was well known to local residents. After due consideration, Sanderson opined that the beast resembled a "donkey-sized dinosaur."[9]

Still, the St. Johns creature excited little comment outside Florida and did not win its now-famous nickname until May 15, 1975, when five boaters near the river's mouth encountered a startling specimen. Witness Dorothy Abram compared the thing to "a dinosaur with its skin pulled back so all the bones were showing . . . [and] pink, sort of the color of boiled shrimp." Its head was the size of a human's or larger, sprouting knobby, snail-like horns or antennae. Its eyes were dark and slanted, while flaps resembling fins or gills dangled below its three-foot-long neck. Companion Brenda Langley agreed with Abram's description, adding that the creature reminded her of a dragon. Journalists dubbed the animal "Pinky," and so it remains, though earlier accounts made no reference to color.[10]

Cryptozoologist Mark Hall, taking his cue from Sanderson, concluded that Pinky must be a relict dinosaur, specifically *Thescelosaurus neglectus*, a relative of the larger *Iguanodon* presumed extinct since the Cretaceous period. Karl Shuker suggests an unknown breed of giant salamander, similar in form and size to China's *Megalobatrachus*, with Pinky's "horns" explained as breathing tubes. Other proposed candidates include a floating log, a large Atlantic sturgeon (*Acipenser oxyrhynchus*), and a Florida manatee (*Trichechus*

Mark Hall suggests that "Pinky" may be a surviving *Iguanodon,* presumed extinct since the Cretaceous period. (Dover Publications.)

manatus latirostris).[11] Admittedly, none of the mundane suspects match the color or specific description of Pinky recorded in 1975, but all share the virtue of being reported from Florida waters.

St. Lucie River

In May 1975, realtor Joan Stoyanoff—wife of renowned Florida architect Dimiter Stoyanoff—sighted a large, unidentified creature swimming along the north fork of the St. Lucie River, in Martin County. She described the beast as thirty feet long and brownish gray in color, but she provided no further details.[12] Correspondence addressed to Mrs. Stoyanoff in preparation for this volume went unanswered. The animal's reported size, if accurate, rules out all crocodilians recognized by modern science.

Gasparilla Lake

In July 2003, several residents of Boca Grande, in Lee County, reported sightings of a dolphin in Gasparilla Lake. Kristine Barr saw the creature every day for two weeks, while lounging on the porch of her lakeside home, and other witnesses confirmed her impression of a marine mammal (family *Delphinidae*) chasing fish across the lake. Tom Farrish, an employee of a local landscaping company, also recorded multiple sightings. Both Barr and Farrish described a small, gray, smooth-skinned creature, two to four feet long, aggressively pursuing fish toward shore.[13]

Since Gasparilla Lake is landlocked, with no access to the nearby Gulf of Mexico, marine mammals of any size are out of place within its waters. Expert Robert Wells discounted the reports, suggesting that misguided witnesses had merely seen an otter or a large fish swimming in the lake. Unconvinced, Kristine Barr replied, "I know how dolphins swim and absolutely it is a dolphin." Tom Farrish, meanwhile, told reporters, "It's like the Loch Ness monster here."[14] And like Scotland's Nessie, the beast remains elusive. No further sightings had been published as of press time for this book.

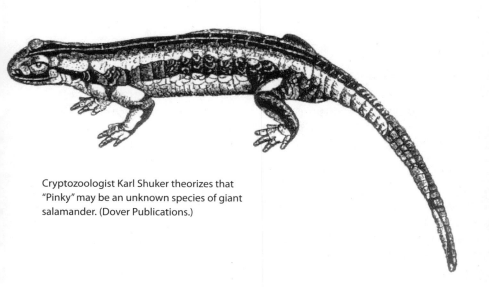

Cryptozoologist Karl Shuker theorizes that "Pinky" may be an unknown species of giant salamander. (Dover Publications.)

6

Old Three-Toes

Between February and October 1948, a remarkable mystery unfolded along Florida's Gulf coast. During that eight-month period, hundreds of large three-toed tracks appeared on beaches and riverbanks at seven locations, on eight separate occasions. They excited local comment, and the rumbles reached New York, prompting a renowned naturalist to investigate. Meanwhile, multiple witnesses reported sightings of large unknown creatures in at least eight separate instances. Police and game wardens confessed their inability to name or trap the beast.

It was, in short, a classic "flap," defined in the cryptozoological literature as a finite series of reports emerging from an area where long-term cryptid sightings are unknown. This time, however, there would be an answer to the riddle . . . but not quite.

The Background

Before examining "Old Three-Toes" in the Sunshine State, we must acknowledge that the mystery did not begin in Florida, in 1948. In fact, throughout the early 1930s, unknown wanderers left three-toed footprints on various beaches from southern New Zealand, to Tasmania and Queensland in Australia, to Argentina, and to Nantucket Island, Massachusetts. In 1937, more tracks appeared with a heap of unidentified feces on a beach in Natal, near South Africa's border with Mozambique. Native witnesses attributed the dung and footprints to reptilian cryptids called *Silwane manzi,* vaguely described as oversized crocodiles with "heads like huge turtles." With DNA testing still fifty years in the future, analysis of the feces by zoologists at Johannesburg's University of Witwatersrand revealed only digested fish. Author Ivan Sanderson, recalling that the first live coelacanth emerged from South African waters in 1938, later suggested that *Silwane manzi* may have been a living dinosaur.[1] No mainstream scientists supported that conclusion, and the global media ignored the 1930s incidents. Today, they seem forgotten for the most part, even among cryptozoologists.

Clearwater and Beyond

No source available today provides specific dates for the original appearance of Old Three-Toes, which was in Pinellas County. Even Sanderson, who documented his investigation of the case in great detail, says merely that the flap began in the predawn hours of a day "in February 1948." Young lovers "smooching" in a car parked near Clearwater's beach approached police at 3:30 a.m., reporting the appearance of "a monster" from the surf. The young man asked patrolmen for a rifle, so that he could shoot the beast. Officers visited the scene, observed a line of three-toed tracks, but took no photographs and made no measurements. In Sanderson's account, the cops and local residents became "well-nigh hysterical" before high tide erased the tracks.[2]

Most published accounts of the Three-Toes affair omit the original eyewitness sighting and skip directly to the subsequent morning, when more tracks appeared at the same location. A half-century after the fact, author Mike Dash claimed that those footprints "came from the sea and marched along the beach for more than two miles before vanishing back into the waves." Sanderson, describing the events in 1948 and afterward, provided no details. Again, it seems that no one photographed or measured any of the tracks (though Dash later referred to plaster casts).[3]

Collection of specific data on the three-toed tracks began on March 6, 1948, when a third set of footprints appeared on a beach one and a half miles north of the original location. The line of tracks traversed one hundred yards of sand. Two weeks later, on March 20, the action shifted to Dan's Island (a part of Sand Key), south of Clearwater Beach. Three-toed footprints marked a beach on the island's north shore, but no other details are known. On April 3, a 350-yard line of footprints appeared at Indian Rocks, ten miles south of the original Clearwater site. Five days later, a full mile of tracks marked a beach three miles south of Indian Rocks Beach. "Some time later," yet another set of tracks surfaced on Tampa Bay, at Philip's Hammock.[4]

The next eyewitness sighting occurred on July 25, 1948. John Milner and George Orfanides, pilot-instructors from the Dunedin Flying School, were flying over the water and saw a large creature swimming two hundred feet offshore from Hog Island (now Caladesi Island), in eight-foot-deep "crystal-clear" water. They judged it to be fifteen feet long, with a "very hairy body, a heavy blunt head and back legs like an alligator but much heavier. The tail [was] long and blunt." Rushing back to the flight school, Milner and Orfanides corralled flight school director Mario Hernandez and Francis Whillock, owner of Clearwater's Beachcomber Restaurant. The four flew back and found the beast again, swimming in eighteen feet of water, traveling at roughly eight knots (9.2 miles per hour). A dozen passes overhead convinced Milner and company that the animal had four limbs, holding the front pair "pressed under the body most of the time."[5]

Another sighting allegedly occurred in August 1948, but it only surfaced after Sanderson published his findings on the case in mid-November. The witnesses, a couple from Milwaukee, wrote to Sanderson that they were fishing from a rowboat north of Tarpon Springs, among the Anclote Keys, when they observed a large gray object on the shore. Mistaking it at first for a tent, the witnesses were startled when the object came alive and waddled toward the surf. They described the creature as "having a head like a rhinoceros but with no neck. It sort of flowed into its narrow shoulders. It was gray and covered with short thick fur. It had short, very thick legs and huge feet, and from its shoulders hung two flippers. It didn't run into the water, or dive in; it sort of slid in half sidewise."[6]

The action moved northward in the autumn of 1948, with two more eyewitness sightings reported "shortly before" the last set of three-toed tracks appeared on October 21. In the first case, witnesses included a Mr. Hayes, deacon of a Baptist church in Chiefland (misspelled "Cheflin" in Sanderson's report), and several others who were picnicking with Hayes. While dining beside the Suwannee River, Hayes and friends observed "a dome-shaped, rough and knobby object," which they mistook for a log until they noticed that it moved upstream, against the current. Rushing to their nearby skiff, the picnickers prepared to follow, but their outboard motor failed to start immediately, and the creature disappeared before they could give chase.[7]

Three days after that undated sighting, a "well-known local character" named Mary Belle Smith observed a similar creature while fishing from the Suwannee's north bank near the point where Highway 19 bridges the river. She described "a very large, dun-colored animal" that surfaced several yards in front of her, which then "paddled" upstream while she watched. Soon after this sighting, nocturnal trapper Martin Sharpe heard "slapping" sounds in a nearby lily pond and rushed to investigate. Before he reached the pond, some unseen creature issued "great gurgling growls" and took off "running or galloping and splashing through the water," leaving Sharpe to conclude that it was "certainly larger than a horse."[8]

The last recorded set of footprints appeared on October 21, 1948, at Suwannee Gables (near Old Town). The trail spanned some two hundred yards, consisting of 242 impressions.[9] Unlike other tracks observed during the flap, they would receive detailed attention from an expert in the field of cryptozoology.

Sanderson Investigates

A native Scotsman, Ivan Terence Sanderson was born in Edinburgh in 1911. He spent his early years in Kenya, on his father's game preserve, before earning master's degrees in botany, geology, and zoology. In the 1930s he led expeditions into some of the world's most remote and forbidding locales, collecting specimens and native tales of exotic creatures that soon filled a series of popular books. Sanderson's zoological titles include *Animal Treasure* (1937), *Caribbean Treasure* (1939), *Animals Nobody Knows* (1940), *Living Treasure* (1941), *Animal Tales* (1946), *Living Mammals of the World* (1955), *Follow the Whale* (1956), *The Monkey Kingdom* (1957), *The Continent We Live On* (1961), *The Dynasty of Abu* (1962), *The Natural Wonders of America* (1962), *Ivan Sanderson's Book of Great Jungles* (1965), and *The USA: This Treasured Land* (1966). His interest also extended to cryptozoology and unsolved mysteries, producing titles that include *Abominable Snowmen* (1961), *Uninvited Visitors* (1967), *"Things"* (1967), *More "Things"* (1969), *Invisible Residents* (1970), and *Investigating the Unexplained* (1972). He founded the Society for the Investigation of the Unexplained in 1965 and led it until his death in February 1973.[10]

Sanderson first heard of Old Three-Toes on July 26, 1948, when reports of the Milner-Orfanides sighting appeared in the *Clearwater Sun* and *St. Petersburg Times*. He followed the case from New York until October, when spokesmen for the National Broadcasting Company (NBC) and the *New York Herald-Tribune* commissioned an on-site investigation. Sanderson then spent two weeks in Florida, examining the latest tracks and interviewing witnesses, afterward producing a fifty-three-page report for his employers and various articles for popular magazines.[11]

Only one set of footprints remained when Sanderson reached Florida, but he made the most of them. After counting the 242 tracks, he measured them precisely, noting that the left foot measured 13.41 inches from its heel to the tip of its clawed middle toe, while the right was 13.5 inches long. The middle toe was longest on each foot, while other heel-to-claw measurements yielded the following results:

Outer toe, left foot—10.24 inches
Inner toe, left foot—10.91 inches
Outer toe, right foot—9.87 inches
Inner toe, right foot—11 inches

The lateral distance between footprints averaged fifteen inches. Calculation of the creature's stride varied by method: five feet between two imprints of the same foot; thirty-one inches from heel to heel of alternating feet; or twenty-five inches "between the heel imprints of two consecutive feet along the base line of direction of the trackmaker's progress." Within those limits, Sanderson found some of the individual footprints turned inward or outward "at strangely incongruous angle[s]."[12]

More fascinating still, in light of later claims that these were man-made, is Sanderson's observation on the depth of the tracks. He wrote:

> The footprints were impressed into the ground to varying depths according to the nature of the soil. . . . [O]ne in soft sand . . . was at least two inches deep all over; those in firm mud were about an inch and a half deep in the middle of the ball of the foot; on loamy soil they appeared to have been pressed to a depth of about three quarters of an inch. . . . We were told by several people who had observed the tracks when fresh—and these included the local police—that the imprints were originally clearly defined on the hardest sand, although we were unable to make any impression on this by stamping *or even by throwing a 35-pound lead model of the imprints down upon it from a height of three feet.*[13] [Emphasis added]

Sanderson consulted unnamed highway engineers, who told him that "[i]f made by a man, either with devices strapped to his feet or on stilts," tracks of the recorded depth would require "a ton on each leg" as the "absolute minimum" weight.[14]

Another argument against man-made tracks was the clear flexibility of individual footprints. Where the prints climbed an embankment, "no heel impressions were left at all but . . . the claws had gouged slots three inches deep on the side of the bank." Elsewhere, in seventeen consecutive footprints, "[m]easurement of the full series . . . showed the following variations in the spread of the tips of the three toes: Left outer to middle toe: 1"; left inner to middle toe: 1½"; right inner to middle toe: none; right middle to outer toe: ½"." Likewise, Sanderson found "that the middle toe could on oc-

Ivan Sanderson suggested that "Old Three-Toes" might be an unknown species of giant penguin. (Dover Publications.)

casion be held up by a root while the outer and inner toes not only reached the ground but gouged deep claw marks into its surface. This is manifestly impossible with any rigid device."[15]

While examining the area, Sanderson himself glimpsed an unknown creature in the Suwannee River, midway between Old Town and the river's mouth. He was airborne with pilot Lloyd Rondeau, in a plane provided by the *Herald-Tribune,* when both saw "some enormous dirty-yellow colored creature rolling about on the surface of the water, making a huge lozenge-shaped patch of foam on the dark waters all around it." Doubling back, they saw no further trace of the beast, which Sanderson said was "about twelve-feet long and four-feet wide, was domed above but had some things at either end which were churning up the water." Finally, two days before Sanderson left Florida (thus, on November 14, 1958), an unnamed witness saw "just the same thing" at Dunedin, ninety-odd miles farther south.[16]

Thus ended Sanderson's investigation, though he never lost interest in Old Three-Toes. In 1967, he suggested that the creature may have been a giant penguin, similar in form to *Palaeondyptes antarcticus,* a seven-foot creature whose fossils are found in New Zealand.[17] Unfortunately, he would not survive to see the riddle "solved," four decades after the fact.

A Hoax Exposed?

In June 1988, fifteen years after Sanderson's death, Florida resident Tony Signorini approached the *St. Petersburg Times* and declared himself responsible for a forty-year-old hoax. According to his story, the discovery of fossil dinosaur tracks in New Mexico inspired Signorini and cohort Al Williams (long since dead) to fabricate a pair of three-toed cast-iron boots, each weighing thirty pounds. Thus shod, Signorini claimed, "I would just swing my leg back and forth and give a big hop. The weight of the feet would carry me. They were heavy enough to sink down in the sand." To cap his tale, Signorini produced the iron feet and posed with them for photographs. Author Mike Dash later reported that "the boots perfectly matched the plaster cast prints taken on Clearwater Beach, proving that the affair was a hoax."[18]

Or was it?

Dash observes that "[t]he whole ridiculous business still has the power to baffle. The principal puzzle is how a naturalist of Sanderson's standing could have allowed himself to be taken in by what was really a rather crude deception." However, while Dash cites one of Sanderson's reports in his notes, he also misstates its contents, claiming that all the tracks "seemed to be made by a jointless, flat-bottomed foot."[19]

In fact, as we have seen, the very opposite was true. The tracks measured by Sanderson in 1948 revealed significant movement by various toes, both laterally and vertically. Likewise, Signorini's iron feet and his method of "hopping" fail to account for the tracks that climbed embankments, digging deeply with the toes and showing no trace of a heel. Finally, we have the evidence of Sanderson's own test with lead casts weighing five pounds more than Signorini's boots, which left no visible impression on the ground beside tracks an inch or more deep.

What of the witnesses, including Sanderson, who claimed sightings of unknown creatures during 1948? Dash mentions only seven of the twenty-odd observers, inflates Sanderson's creature from twelve to twenty feet long, and then dismisses all concerned as liars who "most likely . . . had seen nothing at all," inventing their stories "out of mischief or to please their questioner."[20]

In fairness, it must now be said that questions do remain—not only in regard to Old Three-Toes, but also Signorini's long-delayed confession and the media's uncritical acceptance of his claims.

The Media "Investigates"

Despite its weaknesses—the forty-year delay in "coming clean," discrepancies in size and shape of tracks, the fact that Signorini claimed credit only for the footprints found around Clearwater—journalists worldwide accepted and reported Signorini's tale as fact. Most of them overlooked Sanderson's research, while a few misrepresented its content. In no case was the hoax claim questioned. In the mainstream media today, that the whole thing was a hoax is accepted as established fact.[21]

Determining why this should be the case requires analysis of both the journalists involved and their employers. Most reporters (theoretically, at least) love solving mysteries. Few ever crack a major scandal or expose a sinister conspiracy, but there is pleasure even in small revelations—or debunking local legends. In the higher journalistic ranks, where editors and publishers reside, the daily appetite for news of every sort is never satisfied. If there are no disasters, heinous crimes, or beauty pageants to report, a "silly season" tale of monster-hoaxers may suffice.

All this is not to say that Tony Signorini and Al Williams (who apparently told no one of the hoax before he died) faked no tracks at Clearwater in 1948. They may indeed have done so, though the story told by Signorini raises many questions still unanswered. Nonetheless, there is a history of dubious disclosures in the media where "monsters" are concerned. Two brief examples should suffice to prove the point.

For many years, a black-and-white photograph published in 1934 was widely touted as proof that an unknown, long-necked creature exists in Scotland's Loch Ness. Then, in March 1994, researchers Alastair Boyd and David Martin "exposed" the photo as a hoax. Their proof: the deathbed statement of elderly Christian Spurling, who allegedly built a model monster out of "plastic wood," mounted it atop a clockwork submarine, then persuaded a respected physician to snap the picture and lie about his "sighting." As in Signorini's case, the global media accepted the report without question, declaring the "surgeon's photo" an obvious hoax, collectively wondering how such a transparent fraud had deceived so many gullible "Nessie" investigators for six decades.[22]

Painstaking research by leading cryptozoologists exposed glaring holes in the "hoax" scenario, but their questions were universally ignored by mainstream journalists. First, Spurling's "deathbed" confession was taped in 1991, at least two years before he died. The portrait of a man "clearing his conscience" at death's door was both inaccurate and misleading. Second, Spurling's claim that the photo was snapped in a small Loch Ness inlet is plainly false, as revealed by visible shorelines in the uncropped photograph. Third, the "plastic wood" allegedly employed by Spurling to construct his model did not exist in April 1934. And finally, Spurling's account ignored a *second* photo taken at the same time, rarely published, which reveals the creature's head and neck in a completely different posture, thereby ruling out a rigid model. When asked about that second photo, Boyd and Martin said, "Christian was vague, [he] thought it might have been a piece of wood they were trying out as a monster, but [was] not sure."[23]

A nearly identical media flap occurred in December 2002, following the death of Washington resident Raymond Wallace. Surviving relatives proclaimed him "the inventor of Bigfoot," relating (without proof) how he had faked large footprints in the neighborhood of Bluff Creek, California, during 1958. A subsequent expanded version of the story claimed that Wallace also fabricated ape suits and faked photographs of California's elusive Sasquatch (though again, no proof was forthcoming). By the time a garbled version of the tale reached Scotland, it included claims that Wallace dressed his wife in fur to stage the film of an alleged Sasquatch made by Roger Patterson on October 20, 1967—this was an assertion never made by the Wallace family. As summed up by son Michael Wallace, "Ray L. Wallace was Bigfoot. In reality, Bigfoot just died."[24]

As in the Spurling case, mainstream journalists devoured the Wallace story and beamed it worldwide, adding personal embellishments that exceeded any claims made by the Wallace family. In no case, from Dan Rather to the foreign press, did any "straight" reporter question the family's claims or consult knowledgeable Bigfoot researchers for background information or alternate points of view. If they had done so, the reporters would have learned that Sasquatch sightings date from the early nineteenth century, while Wallace was notorious for his clumsy hoaxes—including absurd tales of Sasquatch captures and extravagant demands for cash in return for ephemeral evidence. No veteran "Bigfooter" took Wallace seriously, in life or death, and he played no role whatsoever in the still-disputed Patterson film of 1967. Indeed, the only mystery for cryptozoologists involved the posthumous attention granted to Wallace years after his last clumsy hoax.[25]

Even the best reporters can be taken in by frauds—witness the CBS debacle surrounding altered military records for George W. Bush in 2004—but most are rightly skeptical when dealing with unsupported assertions. Sadly, that skepticism sometimes fails. The same reporters who might grill and ridicule a Nessie/Bigfoot witness seem incapable of asking the most basic questions when a hoax claim surfaces. That negligence exacerbates misinformation and does nothing to resolve the mystery.

7

Alien Big Cats

In the jargon of cryptozoology, an "alien big cat" (ABC) is any large felid seen, caught, or killed far from its native habitat or in an area where it is deemed extinct. Scientifically, "big cats" (genus *Panthera*) are those possessing a hyoid apparatus that is not completely ossified, enabling the cats to roar while it makes continuous purring impossible. Conversely, "small cats" (genus *Felis*) have a bony hyoid arch that lets them purr while breathing but restricts their hunting calls to high-pitched yowls or screams. Cougars (*Puma concolor*) may rival jaguars and leopards in size, but they are still "small cats" in scientific terms; if sighted far beyond their normal range, however—say in Europe or Australia—they are logged as ABCs.[1]

The Fish and Wildlife Conservation Commission lists three "exotic" cats as recognized in Florida, although the first—*Felis catus,* established in breeding populations for "at least ten years"—is simply a feral version of the common domestic cat. Two South American species, the jaguarundi (*Herpailurus yagouaroundi*) and the ocelot (*Leopardus pardalis*) were initially reported in 1934 and 1958, respectively. Their current status is unknown, but state officials deny that either has a current breeding population. When a Hernando County official reported two jaguarundi sightings in

August 2004, FWCC public information coordinator Karen Parker questioned the witness's credibility. "The jaguarundi I think would be a fascinating story," Parker said, "but from everything I've gathered, I don't think they are here."[2] Whether that judgment is correct or not, some feline mysteries remain within the Sunshine State.

Cougars Astray

Florida presently harbors the only recognized population of cougars (or "panthers") east of the Mississippi River. The subspecies (*Puma concolor coryi*) is endangered, with an estimated seventy adult specimens theoretically confined to the Everglades, Big Cypress National Preserve, and nearby private lands in southwestern Florida.[3] That said, it must be noted that the cats sometimes appear at sites far distant from their shrunken habitat, exciting public comment and some terse denials from state wildlife officers.

Cougars, ostensibly restricted to southern Florida, are nonetheless reported from various other locations. (Dover Publications.)

On March 10, 2003, an unknown motorist struck and killed a cougar near Mango, in Hillsborough County. The hundred-pound cat was Florida's forty-fifth killed in vehicle collisions since 1972, but its passing marked the first appearance of a cougar in Hillsborough County for at least three decades. Five months later and 125 miles farther north, police scrambled in response to another driver's cougar sighting in East Arlington, a Jacksonville suburb. They found no cat on that occasion, nor in September 2003, when hospice director Dan Maison reported a sighting from Stuart. In May 2004, reports of cougar sightings emerged from Volusia County, around Tomoka State Park, though FWCC spokesmen and journalists were generally dismissive. August 2004 brought reported sightings from Brooksville, in Hernando County. Three months later, residents of the Acreage, in Palm Beach County, named a cougar as the unseen predator that scaled six-foot fences to slaughter pets and poultry. FWCC biologists suggested it was a bobcat, instead.[4]

Objections notwithstanding, there could be no doubt about the 125-pound male cougar found dead in June 2005, along the boundary of Flagler and St. Johns counties. Killed by an unknown motorist on I-95, the cat was labeled "UCFP74" (for "un-collared Florida panther"), indicating that the specimen was neither tattooed nor equipped with a transponder chip—in short, a cougar previously unknown to FWCC biologists. No other cougars had been seen in the vicinity for twenty years, and the roadkill left state officials perplexed. Asked if the find meant that other unknown cougars might be prowling the vicinity, Karen Parker replied, "It's definitely a distinct possibility."[5]

Black Panthers

While wandering cougars present a conundrum for FWCC biologists and trackers, at least they represent a species known to inhabit the state. A more complex problem arises with reports of "black panthers" at large in Florida. First, strictly speaking, no such cat exists. The black cats commonly called panthers represent a melanistic form of leopard (*Panthera pardus*) or jaguar (*P. onca*). Of the two, only the jaguar is a native of the Western Hemisphere. Its known range is officially restricted to Mexico and points south, except for two confirmed Arizona sightings in 2001 and 2003.[6]

Whatever their identity in fact, black cats of substantial size have been reported from Florida since 1929, when the first sighting rated a brief mention in *Nature*. Thirty years later, two Fort Myers residents saw a "large, long, black cat" cross the road in front of their car. They further described it as "quite black and very large, much more so than a dog but not necessarily for a panther." John Lutz, founder of the Eastern Puma Research Network, collected 1,683 black panther reports from the eastern United States between 1983 and 2003, including eleven from Florida. FWCC spokesmen assert that no such cats exist within the Sunshine State, but witness Rick Crary disagreed after his Palm City sighting in 2003. In the wake of that encounter, Crary told reporters, "What I saw was not a myth."[7]

Panther sightings are most commonly explained in terms of mistaken identity. Skeptics insist that witnesses have been deceived by shadows or by some familiar species briefly glimpsed in unfamiliar circumstances. Common suspects named (but never caught or photographed to prove the case thus far) include black dogs or feral cats, bobcats, otters, and so on. Melanistic cougars, raised as yet another possibility for panther sightings nationwide, remain undocumented in the scientific literature, though some hunters and game wardens believe such cats exist. If so, zoologist Karl Shuker says, Florida's subtropical forests may offer the ideal natural laboratory to produce a melanistic morph. A third alternative—survival of exotic specimens that have escaped or been released into the wild—finds no support from state biologists or zookeepers, whose specimens, they say, are always safely under lock and key.[8]

Lions at Large

Florida's black panther sightings may be explained by melanistic cougars, or even black dogs glimpsed by nervous witnesses, but the same can hardly be said for reports of male adult lions at large in the state. *Panthera leo*'s size and bushy mane, together with its range of roaring sounds, argue against confusion with known species native to the Sunshine State.

Folklorist Henry Shoemaker, writing in 1917, described a large chocolate-brown cat with a tuft at the tip of its tail (standard with *P. leo* but unknown in cougars), killed at some unspecified Florida location in the early 1900s. A quarter-century and some 180 miles separate Florida's next two lion reports. The second emerged from Loxahatchee on January 23, 1978, when a local resident summoned police to rout the king of beasts from her backyard. Officers arrived too late and failed to meet the cat in their subsequent search of the neighborhood, but inquiries confirmed that no cats were missing from nearby Lion Country Safari or two licensed private menageries.[9]

Police were slow again on November 2, 2003, when residents of Leesburg reported a three-hundred-pound lion prowling their residential neighborhood. Patrolmen searched in vain, then offered a peculiar explanation for the episode. It was a "wild goose chase," they said, beginning when an unnamed woman told neighbors that her "big cat" was lost. The first sighting of a full-grown male lion occurred several hours later, and while officers blamed the reports on mass hysteria, no names or addresses were published to prove a link between the missing house cat and subsequent lion sightings. A parting shot from police headquarters, declaring it "fishy that no one has stepped forward" to claim the alleged lion, applies equally to countless alien big cat sightings throughout the world.[10]

Cryptozoologists Loren Coleman and Mark Hall propose a unique solution for lion *and* black panther sightings throughout the United States. In their view, both cryptids belong to a single species: the Pleistocene predator *Panthera leo atrox,* whose fossils have been found at forty sites between Alaska and Peru (including one in northern Florida). Coleman and Hall suggest that males of the species account for sightings of maned lions in America, while sexual dimorphism produces melanistic females. To support his case, Coleman lists four sightings of maned lions seen *with* "black panthers" between 1948 and 1977. Three other cases, wherein black and tawny cats were seen together, might refer to cougars, if we grant that melanistic specimens exist.[11]

Loren Coleman and Mark Hall hypothesize that Pleistocene cave lions still survive in the United States. (Dover Publications.)

Mainstream scientists dismiss the possibility of prehistoric cats roaming modern America. Cryptozoologist Karl Shuker also challenged the Coleman-Hall theory, noting the "total absence" of reports describing lion prides in the United States. Coleman replies by citing reports from various paleontologists, suggesting that while *P. l. atrox* "may have been social, it did not exist in prides." And in fact, his list of North American lion encounters includes nine sightings of maned males with a single female, the earliest (including three cubs) dating from 1798. In any case, Coleman advances his solution to the mystery as "an intriguing possibility worthy of further exploration."[12] It comes as no surprise, perhaps, that FWCC spokesmen have voiced no interest in pursuing the theory.

Missing Links

Florida's most persistent cryptid also ranks among those deemed by mainstream science as least likely to exist: an unknown primate, said to range in size from four to twelve feet tall. In most reports it is a swamp or forest dweller, but a few have wandered into human settlements. The Seminoles knew it as Esti Capcaki, a cannibal giant of legend. Today, its common nickname is less dignified. Persistent tales of its offensive (even stupefying) body odor brand it the "Skunk Ape."[1]

While every state except Rhode Island has produced reports of unknown hominids or primates, Florida's list of sightings nearly rivals that of the Pacific Northwest, where Bigfoot/Sasquatch has beguiled explorers and researchers since the early nineteenth century. Unfortunately, published sources vary widely in their tabulations of Skunk Ape encounters, while occasional careless duplication and frequent vague references to "several," "multiple," or "numerous" sightings in particular areas frustrate attempts to compile a definitive list. John Green, writing in 1978, counted 104 primate sightings in Florida but failed to give a starting date. Four years later, Colin and Janet Bord listed thirty-two incidents (with one duplicate) between 1947 and 1977. Rick Berry's 1993 list of East Coast primate

Artist's conception of a Bigfoot or Skunk Ape, based on eyewitness descriptions. (Copyright William Rebsamen.)

sightings includes 144 from Florida between 1942 and 1985 (with six duplications and two sightings undated). The Bigfoot Field Researchers Organization (BFRO) reports seventy-three Florida encounters between 1947 and 2004, while the rival Gulf Coast Bigfoot Research Organization (GCBRO) lists thirty-five between 1972 and 2005. My own tabulation, drawing on all of those sources plus various media reports, includes 355 specific Skunk Ape encounters and eleven stories referring to multiple sightings.[2]

Distribution of Skunk Ape sightings is statewide, with reports on file from forty-eight of Florida's sixty-seven counties. Counties with no reports on file include Baker, Bradford, Calhoun, Columbia, De Soto, Franklin, Gilchrist, Glades, Hamilton, Hardee, Indian River, Jefferson, Lafayette, Liberty, Nassau, Sumter, Taylor, Union, and Wakulla. Eleven counties report only one sighting each, while eighteen record five or more. Eight of the latter counties claim Skunk Ape encounters in double digits: Broward (with 15), Collier (36+), Hernando (37–50+), Lee (12), Marion (14), Orange (12), Pasco (15+), and Polk (10).[3]

Previous published accounts date Florida's first Skunk Ape reports from World War II, but newspaper articles retrieved during 2005–6 reveal three "lost" reports from the nineteenth century, including the second-earliest on file for North America, in 1818. Two other accounts date from 1872 and 1900. The next known sighting was logged in 1942, with three reports overall for the 1940s. That incidence doubled in the 1950s and quadrupled in the 1960s, before exploding in the 1970s with at least 166 reported encounters. The 1980s were quiet by comparison, with thirty-eight reports. At least seventy-three reports emerged in the 1990s, while the years 2000–2005 averaged six reports each. Most of the reports on file involve

Skunk Ape sightings multiplied during the 1960s. (Copyright William Rebsamen.)

alleged physical sightings of one or more primates, but several are limited to discovery of large humanoid footprints or unexplained smells and sounds that witnesses associate with previous reports of Skunk Apes in a given area.[4] The space available does not permit a detailed recitation of all alleged Skunk Ape sightings logged within the past sixty-three years, but a review by decades should suffice to place the matter in perspective. (For a list of sightings, see the Appendix.)

Nineteenth-Century Sightings

North America's first supposed primate sighting comes from Maine, vaguely dated in the "early 1800s," and is dismissed by some researchers as fiction. The next on record comes from Apalachicola, in Gulf County, via Scotland's *Edinburgh Advertiser* of July 12, 1818. According to that story, purportedly taken from an undated issue of the *Apalachicola Gazette* that proved irretrievable for this volume, residents of Apalachicola were disturbed by sightings of a five-foot-tall "baboon," pursuing it to a makeshift nest amid cotton bales stored on the north side of town. While the beast "made its scape" and vanished, searchers found many bones nearby, suggesting a carnivorous predator.[5]

Half a century passed before the next Florida incident, again reported from afar by Maine's *Daily Kennebec Journal,* on July 12, 1872. As related in that brief item, a "wild man" was seen picking berries near San Pedro Bay, in Madison County. Witnesses described the visitor as being "entirely covered with hair, and as wild and fleet as a buck." At the approach of humans, it fled swiftly into nearby swamps and vanished. Unnamed locals speculated that their visitor might be a Civil War deserter-turned-hermit.[6]

Finally, September 1900 brought a report from the *Daily Leader* in Davenport, Iowa, detailing more strange events around San Pedro Bay. There, Mrs. Arthur Shiver logged the first sighting of a four-foot-tall biped "covered with short shaggy black hair. Its skin was red and the hair on its head was black and hung below its shoulders. It walked on its feet in a crouching attitude, and held between its legs a sort of stick, which it rode, as children do, dragging one end on the ground. Its arms were long and the fingers looked like claws." Mrs. Shiver summoned neighbors, who pursued the beast but lost it in a nearby swamp. Its six-inch footprints revealed "a claw mark showing that the nail of the big toe was an inch long at least. The other toes protruded and left imprints like sharp claws." Bloodhounds refused to track the beast, but another witness—Bill Went, dwelling beside Canoe Creek—subsequently fired upon it, producing roars of "great rage." Despite "great excitement," hunting parties failed to flush the animal from cover.[7]

The 1940s

Florida's first primate report of the twentieth century also ranks as one of the most dramatic. According to the published versions, a man known only as "Isaac" was driving on a rural road south of Branford (in Suwannee County), sometime in 1942, when a large apelike creature leaped onto the running board of his vehicle. It clung to the car for about half a mile, staring through the window, then dropped back to the ground and fled into the woods. Details are sparse, but one account describes the beast as roughly eight feet tall.[8]

Five years later, a similar creature surfaced at Lakeland, in Polk County. The lone witness, a boy four years old at the time, saw a hairy apelike beast standing among some orange trees behind his home. Twenty years later, memories of the event were clear enough to persuade researcher John Green of the witness's sincerity. A third witness, writing in 2002, informed the BFRO of a sighting near Palatka (in Putnam County) during the summer of 1947 or 1948. The witness, a girl age twelve or thirteen at the time, recalled a "man" covered from head to foot with black hair, apparently scratching its back against a tree trunk. BFRO investigators deemed the witness credible, but granted that she may have seen a bear.[9]

The 1950s

A full decade elapsed before Florida's next primate sighting, in the spring of 1957. Three hunters were camped at some unspecified site in the Big Cypress Swamp—which has been a national preserve since 1974—when they heard heavy footsteps approaching their campsite. After several tense moments, they saw a slump-shouldered figure "too big" to be human watching their camp from the tree line. It studied them in silence for about two minutes, then retreated into darkness, splashing and snapping branches as it went. This sighting may explain another listed on the Internet for 1957, offered without further detail as a report from the Everglades.[10]

Internet sources list three more Skunk Ape sightings from the 1950s, but none provide any substantive detail. The first, reported by an unnamed motorist, occurred somewhere along Highway 46, in Seminole County, during 1958 or 1959. The others, both from 1959, occurred near Apopka (in Orange County) and along the Wekiva River (in Lake County). The three adjacent counties lie roughly one hundred miles north of the Big Cypress Swamp and the Everglades, where 1957's sighting(s) occurred.[11]

The 1960s

While sightings heretofore were isolated incidents, the 1960s produced Florida's first Skunk Ape "flaps." Ten counties were affected, although four—Lee, Orange, Seminole, and St. Lucie—produced only one sighting each. Broward and Charlotte counties produced two sightings each, while Citrus, Hernando, Osceola, and Pasco counties experienced rashes of sightings that sparked "monster" hunts and sensational headlines.[12]

Brooksville, in Hernando County, spawned at least six Skunk Ape reports, though only one is specifically dated. Members of the Lewis family reported two separate sightings of a six-foot, three-hundred-pound primate that visited their mobile home, leaving humanoid footprints behind. Two other reports are so similar that they may represent garbled versions of the same incident (though Rick Berry reports them as separate cases): in both, the witnesses—one male, one female—were changing flat tires when they saw apelike creatures watching nearby. The female witness ("Miss M. B.") logged her report on November 30, 1966, while the male witness's encounter dates vaguely from the "mid-1960s." No details survive for a Brooksville sighting from 1967, but witness "Leon C." allegedly experienced a dramatic encounter two years later, when a large primate pursued and "smacked" his car on Highway 50, west of town. Last, a witness still unnamed reported multiple discoveries of large humanoid footprints in the woods southwest of Brooksville, spanning the years 1969 to 1980. The same witness also blamed Skunk Apes for tearing the roofs off doghouses and savaging a neighbor's livestock, while citing an undated hearsay report of a primate that "played" on a child's swing set.[13]

Holopaw, in Osceola County, produced a flap of sightings in 1963–66, complete with organized hunts and newspaper reports of the elusive (and sometimes aggressive) "Horror of Holopaw." Multiple witnesses reported the beast's first appearance, running across an open field in 1963. One witness, identified only as a "prominent cattleman and citrus grower," told police that "it was definitely an ape of some kind." The animal returned in November 1966, trespassing on the property of Eugene Crosby (some accounts spell it Crosley), allegedly hurling an old tire at him when he approached it on foot. Before year's end, a local ranch hand reported his encounter with a snarling ape that rushed his pickup truck as he sat in a pasture watching cattle pass. Yet another garbled report claims a sighting by (or attack upon) two hunters. Author John Keel claims that the hunters fired on the creature and later found bloodstains in a nearby ransacked "tent house," but no body was recovered. Newspaper reports from the period describe an "Abominable Sandman" five to six feet tall, bipedal, and "twice as broad as a man."[14]

Elfers, near the Anclote River in Pasco County, produced another series of primate reports in the 1960s. Witness Ralph "Bud" Chambers was hiking along the river in the summer of 1966 when he heard loud coughing sounds and saw an apelike creature, seven feet tall and four feet wide, walking upright through the forest. Chambers offered the first published account of the Skunk Ape's "rancid, putrid odor"—a stench so vile, in fact, that when he came back to the site with hunting dogs, the pack refused to trail his quarry. Chambers allegedly met the same creature twice more in 1967, but he had no better luck pursuing it. In January 1967, a smaller primate frightened four teenagers parked on a lover's lane outside Elfers.

As later described to police, the malodorous chimp-sized creature jumped on the hood of their car and stared through the windshield with "glowing" green eyes. They fled in panic from the scene, with nothing but their obvious excitement to substantiate the tale.[15]

Charlotte County produced two Skunk Ape sightings in the 1960s, though one is so garbled in translation that it may refer to another county entirely. The first incident, occurring on August 15, 1962, involved a group of Boy Scouts (Troop 232) camping on the Quedneau Ranch, near Murdoch. High-pitched screams roused them from sleep around midnight, in time to see a "really big, really quick-moving" creature pass their campsite. Author Rick Berry cites a second, undated 1960s report from an anonymous Bull Key fisherman, who claimed repeated sightings of Skunk Ape "families" wading between islands in the "Coya Pelau area." No such place exists in Florida, but there is a Cayo Pelau in Lee County, located near Bull Bay. (In a subsequent listing, Berry also misplaces a 1971 sighting from Big Cypress Swamp at Cayo Pelau, while misspelling the witness's name.)[16]

Two startling encounters emerged from the vicinity of Davie, in Broward County, during 1969. Neither is specifically dated, but both involve "huge" primates seen in orchards by lone witnesses. Charles Robertson was hunting in an abandoned guava orchard, off Road 84, when he met a snarling, smelly primate "over six feet tall." The beast's aggressive demeanor frightened Robertson into dropping his shotgun and fleeing to seek protection from Davie police. Witness Henry Ring's tale was even more remarkable. While hiking through an orange grove, he saw a large black primate treed by dogs. After a moment's hesitation, the creature fled, swinging from tree to tree, and vanished after diving into a canal. Seven years after the fact, both stories were featured in an article published by *Startling Detective* magazine in March 1976.[17]

Near the turn of the twenty-first century, a self-described "43-year-old grandmother" contacted the GCBRO to report a series of Skunk Ape encounters in Citrus County, allegedly occurring between 1969 and 1972. At the time, she resided in a trailer park near an abandoned rock quarry. (No further details of the site's location are available.) As a teen in those days, the witness had spent many weekends at the quarry with her friends, engaged in "partying," but they were often interrupted by night-prowling creatures they called "Blue-eyed Thump Thumps." The beasts were nicknamed for the blue reflection of their eyes by moonlight or automobile head-light beams, and the loud thumping sound of their footsteps. After several encounters—which, surprisingly, never frightened the wit-ness—her companions obtained portable spotlights to illuminate the visitors. The first time they unveiled those lights, the teenag-ers were showered with rocks (none of which found their mark), then glimpsed a "huge hairy creature" scrambling up the quarry wall. Roughly one year later, the young people experienced another spotlight sighting and fired a shot at the creature, without apparent effect.[18]

The remaining 1960s cases are widely scattered and unfortu-nately vague. In the winter of 1962, an unnamed witness glimpsed a Skunk Ape eating guavas outside Hialeah (in Dade County). In the spring of 1963, a nine-year-old child woke from sleep in North Fort Myers (in Lee County) to glimpse a moaning figure "taller than a man" outside his bedroom window. No details survive for a 1966 sighting in Apopka. Three years later, witness Robert Goble saw an eight-foot-tall primate rooting for grubs outside Fort Pierce (in St. Lucie County) and discovered footprints eighteen inches long where it had stood. Before the decade ended, FWCC officers opened a file for Skunk Ape sightings, but few details of those reports ever found their way into print. The most intriguing case of all is remarkably underreported. According to the *Naples Daily News,* one unnamed witness told the FWCC that he had spent six months living with "a family of skunk apes" in the wild. That astounding claim mirrors a 1920s report from British Columbia, but alas, nothing more has yet been revealed.[19]

The 1970s

The next decade produced a veritable explosion of Skunk Ape sight-ings throughout Florida, though many are vague as to dates and de-tails. The year 1970 alone brought sightings from Apopka, Brooks-ville, Geneva, Mims, and the Gulf of Mexico—where a fisherman from Placida (in Charlotte County) allegedly saw an apelike creature swimming twenty miles offshore. All told, the remarkable decade produced at least 166 specific Skunk Ape encounters, plus several nebulous accounts alleging multiple sightings.[20]

The most famous sighting of the early 1970s is also one of the most confused, thanks to careless reporting by various authors. The basic facts are simply told: a party of archaeologists, camped beside an Indian burial mound in the Big Cypress Swamp, were roused from sleep at 3 a.m. when a hairy, foul-smelling primate invaded their camp. They described the beast as eight feet tall and claimed that it left footprints measuring 17.5 inches long and 11 inches wide at the toes. Sadly, authors reporting the case cannot agree if the incident occurred in February 1970 or 1971 (Colin and Janet Bord list it twice in their *Bigfoot Casebook*). They also mangle the surname of the only identified witness, variously calling him "Osbog," "Osborn," and "Osbun." Rick Berry compounds the mystery by placing the incident near Cayo Pelau, some forty miles from the Big Cypress Swamp. Finally, researcher Loren Coleman delivers the coup de grâce with a February 2001 declaration that early 1970s reports from the Big Cypress Swamp were deliberately mislocated "to hide the real locations" of the sightings. (No motive was offered for that supposed disinformation campaign, and my queries to Coleman in October 2005 went unanswered.)[21]

For the remainder of the 1970s, Hernando County led the state in Skunk Ape sightings, with twenty-seven specific incidents on file and one media report claiming "more than fifty." Broward County produced eleven sightings; Lee County residents filed ten reports; Pasco County logged at least eleven; eight emerged from Palm Beach County; Collier, Dade, and Marion counties logged six each; Citrus, Manatee, Polk, and Sarasota counties produced at least five apiece; Charlotte County recorded four sightings; Hendry, Orange, Pinellas, and Putnam counties logged three each; Alachua, Monroe, and Santa Rosa counties each recorded two; while solitary reports emerged from Bay, Duval, Flagler, Hillsborough, Holmes, Lake, Martin, Monroe, and Volusia counties. In seventeen cases, the location was either unrecorded or too vague to permit identification by county (for example, "the Everglades," "Lake Okeechobee," and so on).[22]

Skunk Ape encounters are not restricted to glimpses of dark, shaggy figures. In at least twenty-one cases between 1971 and 1978, unknown primates left footprints in their wake, some of which were photographed or cast in plaster. The first such incident was logged by the archaeologists mentioned above, in the Big Cypress Swamp (or wherever they were). In April 1971, Frank Hudson followed a trail of humanoid tracks through a swamp near St. Petersburg, finally meeting the "huge, hairy creature" that made them. Later that year, outside Davie, witnesses Harry Rose and Joseph Simbili glimpsed a Skunk Ape and found several prints measuring fourteen inches long by ten inches wide. The following year, also at Davie, a farmer found footprints eighteen inches by ten inches near the carcass of a mutilated steer. Police at Immokalee cast a set of fifteen-inch footprints in July 1973. Three months later, on October 24, officers at Hollywood made casts of several three-toed prints measuring fourteen inches by ten. Near the end of 1973, a highway patrolman reported more prints near the scene of yet another Hollywood sighting. Witness Victor Robinson found eighteen-inch prints, with a five-foot stride, at White Horse Key in June 1974. Four months later, a large primate glimpsed by a couple at Brooksville left large tracks behind. The footprints found by Allen Goding at Florida City, in January 1975, measured twelve inches by six (a normal human range). A six-foot-tall "ape" left tracks outside Venice in June 1975. Before year's end, a Polk County hiker found fifteen-inch tracks in an orange grove bordering Green Swamp. Three- and four-toed footprints appeared at Dunnellon in 1976, the latter measuring eighteen inches long. Police in Fort Myers did not count toes on the tracks found in June 1976, but the prints measured two and three inches deep in "wet dirt." The following year, also in Fort Myers, Rick Berry records discovery of tracks "16 × 18 inches." Moon Lake, in Pasco County, produced titanic prints measuring twenty-two by ten inches on April 8, 1977. More modest tracks, thirteen by six inches, surfaced at Nobleton on May 14 and 15, 1977. Gibsonton produced a set of seventeen-inch footprints that same year, while the tracks found at Hudson in June 1978 were simply described as "big."[23]

Another form of evidence—slaughtered pets and livestock—figures in seven Florida Skunk Ape reports from the 1970s. The first such report, from Pinellas Park in 1972, describes a cow killed and mutilated by "something" that left large humanoid footprints. The same year saw a three-hundred-pound steer "torn apart" at Davie, in Broward County, with eighteen-inch footprints found near the carcass. Witness "Mason O." saw a large primate near Brooksville, in February 1973, around the time various "animal deaths" occurred on the same property. Terrance Craigsmith described an incident on January 9, 1974, wherein a hairy "man-like creature" killed a farmer's pony, then leaped a fence and fled with bullets whistling around it. At Lake Worth, in 1974 or 1975, a Skunk Ape allegedly lifted a hundred-pound hog from its pen and bit three large chunks from its flesh before discarding the remains. A Mrs. Morrison of Brooksville recorded multiple Skunk Ape sightings in early 1975, blaming the beast for the deaths of two dogs, twenty-one chickens, and several cattle. Finally, on the night of July 17, 1976, Donald Duncan of Dunnellon fired shots at a primate that grappled with several of his dogs, leaving one with a broken neck and its stomach torn open.[24]

Like other animals, Skunk Apes sometimes appear in groups, characterized by some witnesses as "families." Allen Carter was five years old in May 1972, when he allegedly saw two large primates walking with a "baby" near Brooksville. He summoned relatives, who also saw the creatures and followed their tracks for some distance into the woods. Duane and Ramona Hibner were driving along Highway 476 north of Brooksville on March 11, 1974, when they saw three "man-monkey like creatures" rooting through a roadside garbage heap. In July 1974 or 1975, an unnamed witness met a startling Skunk Ape trio near Lake Worth: the "dad" was silver-gray and twelve feet tall, while the brownish gray "mom" measured eight to ten feet and the "young one" was a mere seven feet tall. In November 1975, John Stohl saw three Skunk Apes in Citrus County, northeast of Homosassa Springs. The largest was approximately eight feet tall, the next largest was a six-foot female

Some witnesses report groups or "families" of Skunk Apes traveling together. (Copyright William Rebsamen.)

with prominent breasts, and the smallest was about five feet tall. An Internet report also claims that Bull Key fishermen have seen "whole families" of Skunk Apes wading between islands "in [the] Coya Pelau [sic] area"—which may, as discussed above, refer to Lee County's Bull Bay.[25]

Skeptics often ask why unknown primates are never struck by cars, yet such reports are not unknown. In fact, Florida drivers allegedly struck Skunk Apes on four separate occasions between January 1974 and March 1976. In the first such case, Richard Lee Smith telephoned the Highway Patrol in Dade County on January 9, 1974, reporting his collision with an eight-foot-tall hairy biped on State Road 27. A subsequent call, recorded in a UPI dispatch, reported that a second motorist had seen the creature limping at the roadside, five miles from the accident site. In January 1975 a female caller told the hosts of a talk show on Miami radio station WFUN that she had struck a Skunk Ape on the Florida Turnpike "three or four months ago." A month later, in February 1975, Steve Voreh allegedly "skidded into" an eight-foot-tall primate on Williston Road, five miles south of Gainesville. When the creature rose again, Voreh says, he shot it four times with a pistol, to no effect. Finally, on the night of March 6, 1976, Steve Humphreys and his wife collided with a "huge" apelike creature at some unspecified point "near Lake Okeechobee." The beast escaped, but their fender was deeply dented. Hair found on the car was reportedly "sent off for analysis," but the rest is silence.[26]

In addition to motor vehicle collisions, Florida residents claimed to have shot Skunk Apes on at least eleven occasions between January 1974 and October 1977. The first such incident involved Fort Lauderdale policeman Robert Hollymeyal, who allegedly wounded a large primate but failed to kill it on January 9, 1974. Nine months later, on September 24, a security guard at a Palm Beach County housing project fired six shots into a smelly seven-foot creature that approached him after nightfall. In November 1974, a group of hunters in Collier County's Corkscrew Swamp peppered a Skunk Ape with shotgun pellets. A Lake Worth witness, who allegedly shot several Skunk Apes at various times during 1974–75, reports that the creatures simply rubbed their wounds and stared at him, perplexed, before fleeing into the woods. Richard Davis fired one shot at a nine-foot primate near Cape Coral on February 2, 1975, then refrained from shooting again because the creature looked "too human." When the animal returned on February 3, Davis changed his mind and shot it again with a .22-caliber pistol. A few days later, the aforementioned Steve Voreh allegedly shot a Skunk Ape near Gainesville, after first striking it with his car. In 1976, a Dunnellon resident claimed that "several people" had fired on the primate that had left three-toed footprints around town. One of those marksmen, the previously mentioned Donald Duncan, fired at the beast that killed one of his dogs on July 17, 1976. On October 3, 1977, Apopka security guard Donnie Hall allegedly shot a ten-foot-tall primate at point-blank range, after it ripped his shirt. The following month, a hunter fired six shots at a Skunk Ape seen near Marion County's Big Scrub Campsites, but the creature escaped.[27]

While witnesses are often frightened by encounters with a Skunk Ape, relatively few report aggressive action on the primate's part. The first report of a Skunk Ape "attack" involves a truck driver sleeping in his cab near Brooksville, where a hairy primate "grabbed" him through the open window, then fled when the trucker cried out. Five years later, in November 1975, witness John Stohl claimed that a Skunk Ape hurled him fifteen feet after he snapped the creature's photograph in Citrus County. (The photo remains as elusive as its subject.) Shortly after midnight on October 24, 1976, an Orlando teenager supposedly met a Skunk Ape in the woods south of town. Surprised, he struck the creature with a stick, then suffered scratches on his left arm when it tried to grab him on the run back to his car. Charles Wilson's guitar practice was interrupted on April 8, 1977, when a hairy biped with twenty-two-inch feet pounded its fists on the wall of his trailer, at Moon Lake. Finally, we have the case of security guard Donnie Hall, who allegedly shot a ten-foot-tall Skunk Ape after it rushed him and ripped off his shirt in Apopka, on October 3, 1977. In no case did the alleged Skunk Ape victims suffer significant injury.[28]

The Skunk Ape found one supporter in the person of Representative Paul Nuckolls, a Republican state legislator from Fort Myers. Twice, in 1976 and 1977, Nuckolls sponsored bills that imposed a one-year jail term and a thousand-dollar fine on anyone who killed one of Florida's unclassified primates. Each time, members of the House Criminal Justice Committee passed the bill, but it failed to reach the floor in 1976 and was reportedly "shouted down" by hostile legislators the following year.[29] Meanwhile, oblivious to the furor in Tallahassee, Skunk Apes continued to surprise and frighten witnesses statewide.

The 1980s

After a hectic decade of close encounters, Skunk Ape sightings declined in frequency over the 1980s, with thirty-eight specific incidents on file and several other vague accounts that defy succinct analysis. Multiple sightings emerged from seven counties, including Lake (five), Hernando (three), Brevard ("several") and Polk ("several"); two sightings each were reported from Collier, Pasco, Sarasota, Seminole, and St. Johns counties; while counties with single sightings included Alachua, Bay, Broward, Charlotte, Citrus, Hillsborough, Levy, Manatee, Orange, Osceola, Putnam, Santa Rosa, and Volusia. Three other reports, from the Big Cypress Preserve and Ocala National Forest, contained no specific mention as to counties.[30]

Sightings from the 1980s mirrored those of previous years, except that no Skunk Apes were reportedly shot or struck by vehicles. Witness Jim Spink allegedly photographed an unknown primate near the mouth of the Peace River (in Charlotte County) on June 12, 1980, later showing his blurry snapshot to a *Miami Herald* reporter, but no trace of the photo remains today. Another curious encounter, reported to the BFRO in May 2001, occurred in Alachua County "around 1985." Witness "M. R.," self-described as "a trained psychologist with a specialty in ready [sic] body language," was strolling near his Alachua home one autumn morning when he spied an ape-like creature "covered with green vegetation" resembling leaves or palm fronds. The sighting was of brief duration, approximately ten to fifteen seconds, and while M. R. insisted that the subject moved "more like an ape than a human," its five- to six-foot height was within human parameters. No other report on file suggests that Skunk Apes may resort to camouflage or may desire to clothe themselves.[31]

Just over two weeks after Jim Spink snapped his supposed Skunk Ape photograph, on June 29, 1980, a contractor working in the Ocala National Forest found a trail of large humanoid footprints near Camp Ocala. Nearby, the witness noted blossoms on surrounding bay trees seemingly devoured. As he followed the tracks, stepping into several of the footprints, the witness allegedly sank hip-deep into muddy soil and was forced to drag himself free by hand. Returning with a friend on June 30, the witness made plaster casts of several footprints measuring 17 inches long by 6.5 inches wide. The unseen walker's stride averaged four feet between prints. An officer of the Lake County Sheriff's Department, Sergeant Dee Kirby, also made casts of the footprints, afterward telling reporters that the tracks "showed a definite arching of the instep, five distinct toes, and even some wrinkling along the instep." While Kirby speculated that the creature might be ten to twelve feet tall and weigh one thousand pounds, Lake County chief investigator

Doug Sewell dismissed the incident as a hoax. As he explained to journalists, "There was no indication that something big enough to make those prints went back through the woods."[32]

The sole alleged report of Skunk Ape aggression from the 1980s emerged more than two decades after the fact, in January 2001. As described to the BFRO by an unnamed female witness, the incident occurred at Plymouth, in northeastern Orange County, during spring 1980. The woman was at home alone when she heard a heavy-footed prowler circling her trailer, fumbling at the door. Alarmed, she grabbed a rifle and waited for the unseen visitor to walk around behind the trailer, then fled into a nearby swamp where she tripped and lost her gun. Glancing back toward the trailer, she "saw Big-foot," then ran to the highway and flagged down a ride. Returning later with friends, the woman found her door ripped from its hinges. She immediately left the property for good, moving in with her sister-in-law.[33]

The 1990s

This decade produced a new surge in Skunk Ape sightings, with at least seventy-three specific reports on file. Collier County led all others, with a minimum of twenty-six sightings plus claims from one researcher of "over seventy" incidents in 1997 alone. Other Florida counties with multiple sightings on file include Osceola (five), Marion (five), Orange (three), and Volusia (three). Two reports each emerged from Brevard, Broward, Duval, Escambia, Jackson, Santa Rosa, and Sarasota counties. Single sightings were recorded from Clay, Dixie, Gadsden, Gulf, Highlands, Lake, Levy, Monroe, Oka-loosa, Palm Beach, Polk, Suwannee, and Walton counties. Additionally, four reports from the Everglades failed to specify a county of occurrence.[34]

Collier County was the seat of Skunk Ape action in the 1990s, be-ginning with an incident on November 20, 1993. Witness "K. R." was hunting with four fellow policemen in a swampy region "between Big Cypress and Alligator Alley" when he found a trail of footprints two or three inches deep, separated by an average six-foot stride. While no one thought to measure the footprints, one witness vid-

eotaped them. That tape has never been broadcast for public viewing and evaluation, but it may be noteworthy that three of the law-
men suspected the tracks were made "by an escaped gorilla." Sadly,
the witnesses provided no further description, leaving researchers
to guess whether or not the tracks included the opposable great toe
seen in normal ape tracks.[35]

Collier County's primate flap of 1997 is less significant for the
number of sightings reported—a figure still disputed—than for
producing the first published Skunk Ape photo and for introduc-
ing Florida's most persistent (and most controversial) "monster"
hunter. Five sightings emerged from Ochopee in the month between
July 16 and August 17, 1997. The first two, on July 16 and 18, were
reported by professional guides Steve Goodbread and Dow Row-
land while conducting groups of tourists on their rounds through
Big Cypress National Preserve. The dozen-odd witnesses to those
encounters agreed that the "ape" stood seven feet tall. Ochopee realtor Jan Brock saw the same beast or its twin on July 21. Within
moments of that sighting, Ochopee fire chief Vince Doerr saw the
creature crossing U.S. Highway 41 and snapped a blurry photograph
of some dark object, seemingly in motion. Researcher David Shealy
heard Doerr's tale and visited the site on July 24, allegedly discovering "several" large footprints. The two prints Shealy cast in plaster
measured 13.5 inches long, six inches wide at the toes, and three
inches wide at the heels. Shealy also claimed discovery of several
brown, three-inch hairs at the scene, but they were subsequently
"lost." A pair of unnamed bird-watchers rounded out the month,
with their sighting of a seven-foot beast whose bulk made it resemble "a linebacker for a football team."[36]

Some observers view David Shealy's role in the Skunk Ape controversy with suspicion. Shealy claimed his first primate sighting in
1973, but he reaped little publicity until 1997, when he lobbied Collier County commissioners to publish Vince Doerr's photo as a tourist draw. By then, Shealy was the proprietor of Ochopee's Florida
Panther Gift Shop (where his Skunk Ape footprint casts reside in a
display case) and the Big Cypress Trail Lakes Campground (scene of
alleged primate sightings and site of Shealy's annual "Skunktober-

fest"). To some, Shealy's marathon pursuit of the Skunk Ape—and its startling results—suggested a small-town P. T. Barnum rather than a scientist. On September 8, 1998, after an eight-month stakeout in his own backyard, Shealy allegedly procured twenty-seven snapshots of an unknown seven-foot primate. If that was not remarkable enough, the beast left four-toed footprints seven inches long and five inches wide at the toes. In August 1999 the Collier County Tourist Development Council approved a forty-four-thousand-dollar tourist-tax grant to fund Shealy's expeditions and "a multilingual Skunk Ape hotline," but county commissioners ve-toed the handout a month later. In July 2000, Shealy borrowed a video camera to tape local wildlife and coincidentally filmed another blurry primate, thereafter calling for laws to protect the Skunk Ape. Critics split between branding Shealy's quest a hoax or an obses-sion. After stints on Comedy Central's *Daily Show*, features on the news-magazine programs *Inside Edition* and *Unsolved Mysteries*, and starring roles in two documentary films, Shealy told the *Naples Daily News* in 2005, "It's not an obsession. But it seems like it's the way my life's come together."[37]

While Collier County claimed most of the media's attention in the 1990s, intriguing reports also emerged from other areas. In June 1991, a Levy County motorist allegedly saw a large primate cross Highway 27 between Bronson and Williston, carrying "a small Bigfoot child." On November 22, 1998, an Osceola County hunter watched two primates—one a female with prominent breasts—cross a road in the Three Lakes Wildlife Management Area. Three sets of alleged Skunk Ape tracks were also reported from Osceola County during early 1999. The first incident occurred in the Three Lakes Wildlife Management Area on January 2, where a hunter first smelled, then saw a primate eight or nine feet tall, weighing an esti-mated four hundred to six hundred pounds. After the beast passed from view, the witness examined its humanoid footprints but took no measurements or photographs. A second hunter in the same vicinity allegedly found similar tracks that same day or the next. Two months later, an unnamed motorist stopping to relieve himself along Nova Road, outside Cocoa, saw a line of six footprints thirteen inches long by eight and a half inches wide. He photographed the tracks and followed them into the nearby woods, where a hog lay dead with its right foreleg "broken and bloody."[38]

Myakka and Beyond

As of press time for this volume, the twenty-first century has produced forty alleged Skunk Ape encounters from twenty-three Florida counties. Counties with multiple reports for the new millennium include Collier (four), Duval (four), Hillsborough (two), Marion (five), Polk (three), and Washington (two). Single encounters were reported from Bay, Dade, Holmes, Lake, Lee, Leon, Okaloosa, Okeechobee, Osceola, Pasco, Santa Rosa, Stark, St. Johns, St. Lucie, Volusia, and Walton counties.[39]

Florida's most sensational Skunk Ape report began unfolding on December 29, 2000, when the Sarasota County Sheriff's Department received a letter postmarked seven days earlier. It read (without grammatical corrections):

Dear Sir or Madam,

Enclosed please find some pictures I took in late September or early Oct. of 2000. My husband says he thinks it is an orangutan. Is someone missing an orangutan? It is hard to judge from the photos how big this orangutan really is. It is in a crouching position in the middle of standing up from where it was sitting. It froze as soon as the flash went off. I didn't even see it as I took the first picture because it was so dark. As soon as the flash went off for the second time it stood up and started to move. I then heard the orangutan walk off into the bushes. From where I was standing, I judge it as being about six and a half feet to seven feet tall in a kneeling position. As soon as I realized how close it was I got back to the house. It had an awful smell that lasted well after it had left my yard. The orangutan was making deep "woomp" noises. It sounded much farther away then it turned out to be. If I had known it was so close to the hedge roll as it was I wouldn't have walked up as close as I did. I'm a senior citizen and if this animal had come out of the hedge roll after me there wasn't a thing I could have done about it. I was about ten foot away from it when it stood up. I'm concerned because my grandchildren like to come down and explore in my back yard. An animal this big could hurt someone seriously. For two nights prior, it had been taking apples that my daughter brought down from up north, off our back porch. These pictures were taken on the third night it had raided my apples. It only came back one more night after that and took some apples that my husband had left out in order to get a better look at it. We left out four apples. I cut two of them in half. The orangutan only took the whole apples. We didn't see it take them. We waited up but eventually had to go to bed. We got a dog back there now and as far as we can tell the orangutan hasn't been back.

Please find out where this animal came from and who it belongs to. It shouldn't be loose like this, someone will get hurt. I called a friend that used to work with animal control back up north and he told us to call the police. I don't want any fuss or people with guns traipsing around behind our house. We live near I75 and I'm afraid this orangutan could cause a serious accident if someone hit it. I once hit a deer that wasn't even a quarter of the size of this animal and totalled my car. At the very least this animal belongs in a place like Bush Gardens where it can be looked after properly. Why haven't people been told that an animal this size is loose? How are people to know how dangerous this could be? If I had known an animal like this was on the loose I wouldn't have aprotched it. I saw on the news that monkeys that get loose can carry Hepatitis and are very dangerous. Please look after this situation. I don't want my backyard to turn into someone else's circus.

God Bless
I prefer to remain anonymous[40]

And to the present day, this witness has remained anonymous. The photos enclosed with the letter appear to show an ape of unknown size and species peering at the camera from behind a screen of palmettos. Sheriff's deputies initially dismissed the letter as a

This photograph of an alleged Skunk Ape accompanied an anonymous letter received by Sarasota County police in December 2000. (Copyright David Barkasy and Loren Coleman.)

hoax, but they passed it along to animal control authorities. One of those officers, in turn, gave photocopies of the pictures to David Barkasy, owner of Sarasota's Silver City Serpentarium. Suspecting that the photos might depict a Skunk Ape, Barkasy alerted cryptozoologist Loren Coleman to the breaking story. Sheriff's officers opened a file for the case on January 18, 2001, regrettably stapling and otherwise damaging the original photos in the process. (Critics later claimed that damage caused by file clerks in the sheriff's office proved the photos were fakes.) Barkasy traced the pictures to a Sarasota photo lab near Interstate Highway 75, where they were printed in December 2000, but the lab's proprietor could not identify the customer who brought the film for processing. There the matter rests for now, with hard lines drawn between critics and supporters of the photos' authenticity.[41]

While skeptics and believers squabbled over the "Myakka photos"—so called for the nearby Myakka State Forest, though nothing proves they were taken there—other witnesses kept on reporting close encounters with Skunk Apes. Six campers blamed the beast for a night of "spine-tingling screams" in April 2000, in the Everglades south of Chokoloskee. One month later, a "giant dark figure" seven to ten feet tall frightened two residents of St. Lucie County. Security guards at Deerwood Park, in Jacksonville, saw an eight-foot-tall primate on four separate occasions between August 22 and September 10, 2000; on September 15, they found a trail of bare footprints that measured twelve inches long and four and a half inches wide (deemed "inconclusive" by BFRO investigators). On September 30, 2000, a Pasco County witness allegedly saw seven Skunk Apes "eating, sleeping and howling" in an orange grove near Dade City. Once again, "large" footprints marked their passing. On New Year's Eve 2001, a shaggy primate interrupted a backyard fireworks display on Tallahassee's east side. Motorists saw a Skunk Ape cross Interstate Highway 10, near Caryville, on February 18, 2003. A year later, on January 18, 2004, a four-foot specimen startled drivers on U.S. Highway 441, in Okeechobee County. On May 16, 2004, an eight-foot primate resembling "a very tall orangutan" frightened a camper in Hillsborough County. On September 6, 2004, five residents of Marion County met a primate as tall as their eight-foot orange tree. The creature glimpsed by a Holmes County witness on July 27, 2004, walked on four thick but "rather long legs," yet the witness insisted it was not a bear.[42]

A Question of Identity

Modern talk-show culture teaches us that many people will humiliate themselves or lie outrageously in the pursuit of profit or celebrity. Bigfoot sightings, photographs, and footprints also have been faked in several states by such notorious hoaxers as Ivan

Marx, Rant Mullens, and Raymond Wallace. Still, even the most dogmatic skeptics grant that some of Florida's Skunk Ape witnesses must have seen, heard, and smelled *something* that they could not explain. Law enforcement officers risk their credibility by reporting encounters with "monsters," and Patrolman Robert Hollymeyal gambled his career by firing on an unknown primate in January 1974. Many civilian witnesses undoubtedly cherish their reputations just as much.[43]

That said, the question still remains: what did they see, hear, or smell? Encounters limited to sounds and odors must be set aside for purposes of our investigation. While alleged Sasquatch cries have been recorded in California and Ohio, analyzed with suggestive but inconclusive results, no such tapes exist in Florida.[44] Various sounds that frighten campers in the Everglades or elsewhere may originate with cougars, birds, or other species known to science but unrecognizable to the "earwitnesses." The same is true for various accounts of "heavy footsteps," snapping branches, and the like, where no Skunk Ape was seen. Likewise, foul odors by themselves may rise from rotting carcasses or vegetation, swamp gas, stagnant water, sewage, mineral deposits, and so forth.

Footprints alone are also problematical. While some reported from Florida (and cited above) clearly fall outside the normal human range of sizes, skeptics argue that all such are fakes. Western researchers answer that challenge with forensic lab reports describing humanoid dermal ridges found on footprint casts from California and Washington. No such detailed prints have yet been cast in Florida, although one set of tracks from Lake County (discussed above) displayed "some wrinkling along the instep." Meanwhile, no three- or four-toed apes are known to science. Most serious researchers today regard as fakes the three-toed footprints cast in 1974 in Louisiana's Honey Island Swamp.[45] As it stands today, footprints only qualify as evidence when coupled with a sighting of the beast itself.

But evidence of *what?*

While skeptics acknowledge the sincerity of Skunk Ape witnesses, they commonly explain such sightings as mistaken identity and exaggeration. Some of the figures logged as "unknown" in the records may in fact be human beings. A case in point involves the creature with a "cave man type face," dressed in "dirty torn clothes," glimpsed by two witnesses driving through Putnam County in the foggy predawn hours of a summer night, in 1971 or 1972. While the figure's visible flesh seemed "very hairy," still the observers described it as resembling "a man more than an animal." Its reported size—six and a half to seven feet tall, "around 270 or more pounds"—fits human parameters, with an allowance for surprise, poor visibility, and subsequent exaggeration. (The report was not filed with BFRO investigators until January 2001.) And no doubt remains in the case of one "creature" reported from Green Swamp during 1991 and 1992: authorities captured a Taiwanese sailor, Hu Tu Mei, who escaped from Tampa General Hospital's psychiatric ward and lived in the swamp for nearly eight months, alarming several witnesses with his wild appearance.[46]

Misidentification of known animals is another frequent explanation for hominid sightings, from Yeti in the Himalayas to Sasquatch in the Pacific Northwest. Skeptics note that bears often stand erect and may also walk on their hind legs (albeit awkwardly, for short distances). Florida presently hosts some two thousand black bears (*Ursus americanus floridanus*), dwelling in the Apalachicola National Forest, Big Cypress National Preserve, Ocala National Forest, the Osceola National Forest, and the Wekiva River Bottoms—all sources of multiple Skunk Ape reports. Bears suffering from mange have also been advanced as possible Skunk Ape suspects, including the case of a supposed primate that "flashed" two female Swedish tourists near Ochopee, in February 2003. David Shealy opined that it was "almost Skunk Ape mating season and the creatures are attracted to the scent of menstruation"—a fact also noted for bears.[47]

Escaped pets, zoo specimens, or circus animals are frequently suggested to explain cryptid sightings, and the Skunk Ape is no exception. Ivan Sanderson reported that a young orangutan escaped in 1954, while in transit to an unnamed "well-known Florida organization," but he withheld further details since the animal had been reported dead in an apparent case of insurance fraud. George Eberhart also suggests an escaped chimpanzee, while admitting that no such escapes are on record in Florida. Certainly there are no cases of escaped gorillas, and none of Florida's acknowledged exotic primate species come close to the size of even the smallest reported Skunk Apes. Exaggeration may be granted in some cryptid reports, but even the most timid witness seems unlikely to mistake a rhesus or squirrel monkey for a hulking eight-foot ape.[48]

Indeed, no primate living resembles the seven- to twelve-foot behemoths described by witnesses in Florida and throughout the world at large. The only candidate of such dimensions, *Gigantopithecus blacki,* lived in Southeast Asia from the Miocene epoch to the Middle Pleistocene, when *Homo erectus* invaded the huge ape's domain. Presumed extinct for some eight hundred thousand years, "Giganto" is known only from a handful of teeth found in China. No current evidence suggests that it reached the Western Hemisphere, although some cryptozoologists consider it a candidate for both the Himalayan Yeti and North America's Sasquatch. Any link to prehistoric Florida, much less to the present-day Sunshine State, is purely speculative.[49]

The paucity of living Bigfoot/Skunk Ape candidates has prompted cryptozoologists to hypothesize whole family trees of unknown hominids and primates. Ivan Sanderson was the first to propose such a classification system, in 1961. His four categories included "sub-humans" (presumed to be surviving specimens of *Homo neanderthalensis*), "proto-pygmies" (including all the smaller unknown primates worldwide), "neo-giants" (identical to *Gigantopithecus*), and "sub-hominids" ("in every way the least human"). Four decades later, Mark Hall proposed four categories of his own: "shorter hominids" (analogous to Sanderson's "sub-humans"), "least hominids" (relict populations of *Homo erectus*), "taller hominids" (including possible survivors of *Homo gardarensis* and *H. sapiens rhodesiensis*), and "true giants" (an evolved form of *Gigantopithecus*). In 1999, authors Loren Coleman and Patrick Huyghe advanced a staggering nine categories of unclassified primates, including "neo giants" (relict specimens of *Gigantopithecus* or *Paranthropus robustus*), "true giants" (another version of *Gigantopithecus,* this one with four-toed feet), "marked hominids" (large primates with piebald coloration), "Neandertaloids" (analogous to Sanderson's "sub-humans" and

Hall's shorter hominids), "erectus hominids" (identical to Hall's second category), "proto-pygmies" (borrowed from Sanderson), "unknown pongids" (a group of as-yet-unclassified apes), "giant monkeys," and "merbeings" (an amphibious class, unaccountably including El Chupacabra).[50]

It need hardly be said that mainstream scientists reject out of hand all such speculative species and suggestions of prehistoric survivors. That rejection, while reasonable on its face, does nothing to resolve the mystery of Florida's elusive (or illusory) Skunk Ape.

Stranger Still

Thus far we have examined cryptids either by their class ("sea serpents," lake "monsters," alien big cats, and unknown hominids) or by specific cases (*Octopus giganteus* and Old Three-Toes). This chapter scrutinizes those that fail to meet the previous criteria, either because they are so strange as to defy ready classification, or because the information presently available does not include sufficient detail for analysis. That said, no tour of the state's elusive denizens would be complete without some mention of the beasts considered here.

Big Birds

Reports of massive "thunderbirds" constitute a major vein of aboriginal mythology in North America. Additionally, sightings of birds resembling giant eagles have emerged from various locations over the past forty years, including reports and occasional blurry photographs from Alaska through the Midwest, to Texas and West Virginia. George Eberhart lists three such sightings from southern

Florida—at Matheson Hammock Park, Sand Key, and along the Tamiami Trail—but he provides no dates or other details. According to thunderbird researcher Mark Hall, the Tamiami Trail specimen, reported in 1961 by an author who "had a poor record for getting the details correct," was described as a "giant vulture" with a fifty-foot wingspan. Yet another report of "something in flight . . . many years ago around Tallahassee" is too vague for serious consideration here.[1]

Hall suggests that both ancient and modern thunderbird sightings may be explained by survival of a prehistoric raptor, *Argentavis magnificens,* whose fossil remains have been excavated from Late Miocene deposits in Argentina. The bird, presumed extinct for some five million years, weighed 158 pounds and boasted a wingspan of twenty-five feet. Two smaller relatives from North America, *Teratornis incrediblis* and *T. merriami* (both likewise presumed extinct), had wingspans of nineteen and twelve feet, respectively. More prosaic candidates include the golden eagle (with a seven-foot wingspan), the turkey vulture (six feet), and the black vulture (five feet across).[2] None of the latter birds approach the size reported by "big bird" eyewitnesses, but exaggeration may account for the discrepancy.

A very different giant bird was once reported from Daytona Beach, in an undated incident that strains credulity. Charlie Carlson's "Strange Florida" Web site relates that an unnamed male witness saw a bird resembling a huge chicken, some twenty-five feet tall, standing on the corner of a residential street. As if that was not strange enough, the witness claimed that the bird was "identical to another giant chicken" he saw in Michigan, before moving to Florida—except that the Daytona bird wore "polka-dotted underwear"! No bird of that size is known to modern science, either living or from fossil forms, although an eight-foot flightless specimen (*Titanis walleri*) inhabited North America through the late Pleistocene epoch.[3] Logic dictates that the Daytona Beach sighting belongs more properly to a study of mental illness or substance abuse, than to cryptozoology.

A Flying Serpent

Our sole report of a huge winged reptile soaring over southern Florida comes fourth-hand from the *Daily Iowa Press* of June 15, 1899. According to that story,

> Policeman O'Brien of New York has received a letter from a friend in Everglades, Fla., describing a monster seen there recently. O'Brien's correspondent calls the thing a "flying snake." He says it was first seen by the McCorkle brothers, whom O'Brien knows well, as they were walking through their orange grove. "The snake rose from the top of an old orange tree," says the writer, "and started circling westward. It was about thirty-five feet long and had four wings, a skull like a puff adder, a bald pate, tapering tail, eyes that flashed fire, a tongue that was plainly venomous, and a look of dark blue annoyance." O'Brien's correspondent adds that the sober citizens of the place had formed a hunt club and are making plans to bag the snake.[4]

We may assume from lack of any further correspondence that the hunt proved fruitless.

Unicorns

Although less famous than his cousin Sir Francis Drake, Sir John Hawkins also made his mark in New World exploration during the sixteenth century. Describing his voyage of 1564, Hawkins wrote:

> The Floridians have pieces of unicorne hornes which they wear about their necks, whereof Frenchmen obtained many pieces. Of those unicornes they have many; for that they doe affirme it to be a beast with one horne, which coming to the river to drinke, putteth the same into the water before he drinketh. Of this unicornes horne there are of our company, that have gotten the same of the Frenchmen, brought home thereof to shew.[5]

Sir John Hawkins claimed that unicorns inhabited Florida in 1564. (Dover Publications.)

A marginal note in the text refers further to "Unicorne hornes, which ye inhabitants call Souanamma." Researchers thus far have failed to link that name to any creature living or extinct, and while George Eberhart suggests the moose (*Alces alces*) as a candidate for unicorn reports from Canada and Maine, no corresponding ungulate is found in Florida.[6]

A Mermaid

This peculiar story differs from our other reports in that it describes not a sighting, but the *capture* of an unknown creature. Once again, however, the report comes not from Florida, but from paper published in Ohio, the *Marion Daily Star* of May 13, 1890.

According to that story, one W. W. Stanton, a mate aboard the schooner *Addie Schaeffer,* netted a unique catch while fishing on April 29, three hundred miles off the coast of St. Augustine. According to the *Daily Star*'s reporter in Jacksonville,

> This strange creature is about six feet long, pure white and scaleless. The head and face are wonderfully human in shape

and feature. The shoulders are well outlined, and very much resemble those of a woman, and the bosom is well defined and shows considerable development, while the hips and abdomen continue the human appearance. There are four flippers, two of which are placed at the lower termination of the body, and give one the impression that nature made an effort to supply the strange creature with lower limbs. Mr. Stanton confesses to quite a fright on first sight of his queer prize, which, on being drawn on board, gave utterance to a low, moaning sound, which might easily have been mistaken for the sobbing of a baby.[7]

The anonymous scribe claims no glimpse of the creature, which reportedly died two days after its capture, but he or she describes the *Addie Schaeffer* "thronged all day" by locals anxious to see the curiosity preserved in "a large six foot glass of alcohol." The report concludes that Stanton, "after visiting several ports and showing his queer creature, will donate it to the Smithsonian Institution"—which never received it.[8]

Pink Alligators

Two crocodilian species, the American alligator (*Alligator mississippiensis*) and the American crocodile (*Crocodylus acutus*) are native to Florida. FWCC spokesmen also recognize an exotic species, the spectacled caiman (*Caiman crocodilus*), as established in the state and breeding in the wild. Despite variations in length and the shape of their heads, all three are similar in appearance, with colors ranging from greenish gray to black.[9] None match the physical description of the reptile seen in the Everglades, near Andytown, in early March 1976.

Professional guide Danny Decker reported two sightings of a pink alligator in a canal outside Andytown, occurring on March 3 and 4, 1976. No other witnesses were present, and his story prompted the expected jibes about intoxication, but George Eberhart suggests two alternate explanations. First, an albino or leucistic alligator, although nearly white in color, might seem pink in certain lighting or when viewed through dirty water. Second, Eberhart observes that young spectacled caimans are yellowish in color, and might likewise seem pink in less than optimal viewing conditions. Whatever the true explanation, Decker's sightings on successive days marked the first and last appearance of Florida's alleged pink alligator.[10]

A Phantom Kangaroo

Throughout North America, from 1899 through 2005, residents of at least eighteen states and two Canadian provinces have reported sightings of kangaroos at large. One peculiar specimen allegedly "killed dogs right and left" around South Pittsburgh, Tennessee, in January 1934. Illinois police spent a month chasing elusive marsupials through Chicago and South Plano, in the autumn of 1974.

A phantom kangaroo allegedly visited Florida in 2002. (Dover Publications.)

Two years later, another misplaced kangaroo outran five officers in Golden, Colorado. In no recorded case were any kangaroos or wallabies reported missing from a local circus, zoo, or private menagerie.[11]

In December 2002, researcher Chad Arment published the anonymous, undated account of a witness who allegedly sighted a peculiar beast, described as "a cross between a rat and a kangaroo," at some undisclosed location in Florida. The animal, seen from fifty yards away, was gray in color, thirty to thirty-six inches tall, and while resembling a kangaroo in all significant particulars, it "scampered on all fours." After perusal of the Internet, the nameless witness concluded that the beast most closely resembled a Bennett's wallaby (*Macropus rufogriseus fruticus*). Arment notes that wallabies are "fairly common" as exotic pets in North America, while feral colonies are recognized in Britain and Hawaii.[12]

Loren Coleman, after three decades of research on the "phantom kangaroo" phenomenon, suggests a more surprising explanation. In his view, while some reported sightings may involve actual kangaroos or wallabies at large, other cases are explained by sightings of large, unclassified "devil monkeys." While the FWCC acknowledges several exotic primate species breeding in Florida, none is large enough to be mistaken for a kangaroo.[13]

Giant Armadillos

In October 2001, researcher Brad LaGrange published the story of a witness identified only as "Jane," relating her encounter with several "really large armadillos" in an orange grove near Tampa, sometime in the early 1970s. Roused from sleep late one night by "snuffling" or "rooting" sounds outside her home, Jane followed the noise into the nearby orchard and found several large creatures digging in the soil. Their pointed ears, slim tails, and "armored" backs reminded her of armadillos she had seen in other states, but these specimens measured four to five feet long (tails included). The animals returned several times over the next two weeks, witnessed by other members of Jane's family, but in their ignorance of local wildlife, the observers "didn't think too much of it."[14]

A witness claims to have seen giant armadillos near Tampa in the early 1970s. (Dover Publications.)

LaGrange notes that Florida harbored seven-foot armadillos (*Holmesina septentrionalis*) during the Pleistocene epoch, but he considers exotic introduction of modern South American giant armadillos (*Priodontes maximus*) a more likely explanation for Jane's sighting. Specimens of *P. maximus* may exceed three feet in length and weigh close to sixty pounds at maturity. The FWCC acknowledges no such imports, but admits that the much smaller nine-banded armadillo (*Dasypus novemcinctus*) has been established as an exotic species in Florida since the 1920s.[15] Whichever armadillos Jane encountered, surprise and the passage of three decades may account for exaggerations in size.

El Chupacabra

Our last supposed cryptid is doubly exotic—not only a species unrecognized by science, but a foreign import as well. The Chupacabra ("the goat sucker") was reported first from Puerto Rico during March 1975. The creature earned its name by savaging livestock and leaving the carcasses drained of blood. The attacks spread to Guatemala in November 1995, then to Mexico in February 1996, and reached U.S. soil for the first time with reports from Florida in March 1996.[16]

Sweetwater resident Teide Carballo logged the state's first Chupacabra report on March 10, 1996, after watching an "inhuman shape" cross her yard. The following night, a witness in Miami's Little Havana district found several chickens dead in their cage and watched a dark form "neither human nor simian" duck out of sight in some nearby foliage. Alleged three-toed footprints found at the scene measured five inches long and four and a half inches wide. Two weeks after that attack, Olimpia Govea found two goats and twenty-seven chickens slaughtered on her Sweetwater property by an unseen predator that drained the carcasses of blood. Another Sweetwater neighbor, Barbara Martinez, lost more than forty birds, apparently killed outside her open bedroom window while she slept. The last recorded attack, claiming a dozen sheep and goats, occurred in Hialeah Gardens on May 2, 1996, at the home of Rafael Moreno. Authorities blamed the raids on stray dogs (which are not known to drink blood while leaving the flesh of their prey), while Miami merchants took the scare in stride. T-shirts appeared with monstrous pictures of the Chupacabra, a local diner hawked "Chupacabras sandwiches," and another restaurant changed its name to El Chupa Cabra.[17]

Thus ended Florida's brief monster panic, although reported sightings and attacks continue to the present day in Puerto Rico, Texas, Argentina, Chile, Guatemala, and Nicaragua. Witnesses outside of Florida commonly describe the Chupacabra as a biped four to five feet tall, covered in short gray fur, with large red eyes, prominent fangs, and a row of spikes or spines running along its back.

Aside from feral dogs, George Eberhart suggests attacks by weasels, monkeys, and vampire bats to explain Chupacabra predation in Puerto Rico and Latin America. None of those suspects seems likely in Florida, and claims of mass hysteria (while perhaps accounting for certain eyewitness descriptions) does not explain the death of animals found drained of blood. Possible culprits in that regard include Santería cultists or other dabblers in the occult who perform blood sacrifices.[18]

Conclusion

Where Be Monsters?

Hidden animals, by definition, need somewhere to hide. Our final mission, then, is to discover whether modern Florida accommodates that need, or if its landscape is so well explored, so fully occupied, that any claim of living cryptids must be taken as a hoax or case of simple error.

In 1812, Baron Georges Cuvier—an esteemed French zoologist and the "father of paleontology"—declared, "There is little hope of discovering new species of large quadrupeds." With regard to ongoing reports of "sea serpents," Cuvier added, "I hope nobody will ever seriously look for them in nature; one could as well search for the animals of Daniel or for the beast of the Apocalypse." Seven years later, two of Cuvier's students surprised him by discovering the American tapir. Since his death in 1832, a random sampling of zoological discoveries includes the lowland gorilla (1847), the pygmy hippopotamus (1870), Cotton's white rhinoceros (1900), the okapi (1901), the mountain gorilla (1902), the giant forest hog (1904), Dawson's caribou (1908), the Komodo dragon (1912), the kouprey (1937), the saola (1992), the giant muntjac (1994), and the leaf muntjac (1997). At sea, discoveries undreamed of by Cuvier include

The okapi (left) and muntjac are two of many new species discovered during the twentieth century. (Copyright William Rebsamen.)

sixteen species of whales (1827–1913), the whale shark (1828), the giant squid (1857), living coelacanths (1938), and the megamouth shark (1976). In fact, science recognized only 5,738 animal species when Cuvier penned his premature warning; by 2000, the list had grown to 1.8 million species.[1]

Florida, of course, is not some "Third World" nation where vast tracts of jungle stand virtually unexplored until logging crews come to destroy them forever. The 2000 census found 15,982,378 year-round residents in Florida, and this number had increased by 2003 to an estimated 17,019,068. That amounted to 296.4 persons per square mile, occupying 7,624,378 housing units. Furthermore, 74.6 million tourists visited the Sunshine State in 2003, a number that increased to 79.8 million in 2004.[2] Surely, no unknown beasts of any size could hide in such a bustling, crowded state.

That picture changes somewhat when we recognize that some 96 percent of Florida's full-time residents live in just forty-three cities, concentrated along the Atlantic and Gulf coasts. Indeed, some 39 percent of the state's official population resides within just four cities: Fort Lauderdale, Jacksonville, Miami, and Orlando. Miami alone claims as many residents as forty-three of Florida's other sixty-six counties combined.[3] Clearly, then, the state is not as densely populated as extrapolation of statistics might suggest. It now remains for us to survey places where elusive cryptids might conceal themselves, and we begin where life itself began—offshore.

The Sea

No one today pretends that science has discovered, classified, and cataloged all marine species on earth. During the years 2000 through 2002, the Census of Marine Life listed five hundred new species of fish. In 2004, researchers found twelve new species off the coast of Panglao, in the Philippines. In 2001, marine biologist Charles Paxton speculated that fifty or more marine species greater than six feet in length still awaited discovery.[4]

It should be no great wonder, then, if unknown creatures are observed or found beached along Florida's shores. Curiously, published measurements of the states's total coastline vary radically, including reports of 1,197 miles, 1,350 miles, and 8,246 miles. The latter figure, cited by FWCC spokesmen, represents total miles of tidal coastline patrolled by state conservation officers, presumably including Florida's forty-five hundred islands exceeding ten acres in size (a statistic bested only by Alaska).[5] While speculation concerning future "sea serpent" sightings or strandings is fruitless, Florida's beachcombers, boaters, divers, fishermen, surfers, and swimmers obviously have *some* chance of spotting unknown animals at sea. More systematic searches might reward cryptozoologists with creatures great or small.

Freshwater Species

Some 5,983 square miles of the Sunshine State lie underwater. Florida boasts more than seventy-seven hundred lakes—more than any other state—plus thousands of ponds, rivers, creeks, streams, and canals. Some of the lakes are still unnamed. They range in size from one acre to 448,000 acres (Lake Okeechobee, America's second-largest freshwater lake), and a total of 115 Florida lakes exceed 1,000 acres in size. Florida's longest river, the St. Johns, flows northward over 310 miles. Other significant rivers include the Apalachicola, Caloosahatchee, Indian, Kissimmee, St. Marys, Suwannee, and Withlacoochee. Each year, FWCC conservation officers patrol three million acres of lakes and ponds, twelve thousand miles of rivers and streams, and eleven thousand miles of canals. All told, they estimate that Florida harbors 208 species of recognized freshwater fish.[6]

But is that census complete?

As with the sea, no one should be astounded if Florida's freshwater realms yielded new species of fish, reptiles, or amphibians in years to come. It *would* be startling if a giant penguin or pink dinosaur emerged to favor tourists with a photo opportunity, but there may be surprises yet in store for researchers throughout the Sunshine State. The possibilities, while clearly not unlimited, remain encouraging for both professional and amateur investigators.

Swamps and Marshes

Swamps bridge the gap between freshwater and dry land in Florida, providing a rich and diverse habitat for wildlife of all kinds. Only four of Florida's sixty-seven counties (Clay, Gadsden, Palm Beach, and Sarasota) claim no swamps, while the other sixty-three boast 1,032 identified by name. The boggiest counties include Jackson (with 88 swamps), Holmes (77), Washington (71), Collier (45), Lafay-

Florida's swamps have produced the majority of Skunk Ape sightings. (Copyright William Rebsamen.)

ette (35), Liberty (34), Lake (33), Hamilton (32), Osceola (30), Volusia (29), Walton (29), Calhoun (26), Sumter (25), and Baker (24).[7]

Scientifically speaking, Florida's marshlands are classified either as river swamps (dependent on rivers for their water) or still-water swamps (fed by ground seepage and rainfall). That distinction, while critical for plant life and some small aquatic species, is irrelevant with respect to pursuit of ABCs, Skunk Apes, or other terrestrial cryptids. More important is the physical extent of Florida marshlands, wherein human habitation is restricted and travel often cumbersome at best. Florida's largest swamp, the Everglades, covers some 4,500 square miles. The Big Cypress Preserve spans 2,400 square miles, while the Green Swamp sprawls over 870 square miles and the Okefenokee (shared with southeastern Georgia) covers another 700 square miles.[8] Again, it comes as no surprise that these wild regions produce a disproportionate number of unknown primate sightings.

Consider the impact of Florida's swamps on the distribution of her human population. While brochures and Web sites claim an average distribution of 296.4 persons per square mile, a closer look reveals significant discrepancies. The state's five least-populous counties include Glades (with 10,576 residents), Gulf (13,332), Jefferson (12,902), Lafayette (7,022), and Liberty (7,021). In population density, they rank as follows: Liberty, 8.4 persons per square mile; Lafayette, 12.9; Gulf, 17.4; Glades, 18.9; and Jefferson, 21.2. Even then, the distribution figures paint a false picture, since Lafayette County has 35 virtually uninhabited swamps, Liberty has 34, Gulf has 18, while Jefferson and Glades have 6 and 5, respectively. Collier County, the state's epicenter of Skunk Ape reports, ostensibly harbors 143.7 persons per square mile, but a glance at the map reminds us that the county's vast swampland restricts most human inhabitants to the coastline or scattered outposts along State Highway 29. Most of Collier's 1,994 square miles are as wild today as they were in the nineteenth century.[9]

What dwells within those vast, forbidding swamps? We have examined some of the exotic species breeding there, including large reptiles introduced from South America and Asia. Florida's last bears and panthers cling to life within those wetlands, and it may not be too much to hope that other species yet unclassified share portions of their habitat. Only further research—or possibly a case of pure, dumb luck—will finally resolve that question.

Dry Land

I use *dry land* advisedly, since large tracts of Florida forests and bottomlands are subject to seasonal flooding, periodically transformed into swamps. As in the case of Florida's coastline, various sources disagree on the state's total area, offering figures between 58,560 square miles (54,252 of dry land) and 59,909 (with 53,927 above water). FWCC officers reportedly patrol more than 57,800 square miles of public and private land in any given year, including the Apalachicola National Forest (882 square miles), the Ocala National Forest (450 square miles), the Osceola National Forest (312 square miles), and the Withlacoochee State Forest (246 square miles). Wet or dry, while dwarfed by the jungles of Brazil or the forests of the Pacific Northwest, Florida's untamed lands still harbor 672 recognized species of wildlife—and perhaps a good deal more.[10]

Forests throughout the Sunshine State also harbor their share of mysteries. (Copyright William Rebsamen.)

The Quest

No one has yet devised a surefire method for procuring cryptids in the flesh or proof of their existence in the wild. Concerted, systematic searching resurrected the ivory-billed woodpecker from extinction in 2005, but such efforts require dedicated personnel, equipment, and funding unavailable to most amateur cryptozoologists. Hunters such as Peter Byrne and René Dahinden devoted lifetimes to the pursuit of Sasquatch without bagging their quarry; a few, like Jordi Magraner—murdered in Pakistan while stalking an elusive primate—have sacrificed their last breath to the quest. Oilman Tom Slick's millions failed to unmask either Yeti or Sasquatch, despite repeated efforts with teams of professional trackers. Conversely, in 2002 a simple camera "trap" documented the survival of at least one Arizona jaguar (*Panthera onca arizonensis*), presumed extinct since 1905.[11]

Those photos were accepted as evidence primarily because the jaguar, while believed extinct within its former range, was yet a species recognized by science. Conversely, alleged photos, motion picture films, and videotapes of various unknown primates, lake "monsters," or "sea serpents" face overwhelming skepticism—with good reason, in the case of certain clumsy fakes—and will never stand alone as proof of any cryptid's physical existence. Photographic trickery is far too commonplace in the computer age for any mainstream scientist to grant that images on film are proof of anything. Likewise, even the most meticulously detailed footprint casts may theoretically be faked, assuming that their purveyor possesses all the knowledge, skill, and tools required to perpetrate a lifelike hoax.

That stalemate has produced a sometimes bitter rift within the cryptozoological community. Some researchers contend that only a type specimen will prove their case, insisting that a cryptid must be caged or killed to satisfy the doubters—and, perhaps, to win legal protection for the species. Dr. Grover Krantz, of Washington State University, argued long and hard from 1968 until his death in 2002 that Sasquatch should be shot on sight to prove and preserve its existence. Peter Byrne denounced Krantz's plan as "criminal and unnecessary," complaining that the first creature gunned down might be "the last one." Krantz replied that if the species was endangered, proving its existence with a single kill was all the more imperative, since "the government is going to pay no attention and do nothing to help unless you prove the animal exists." Thus far, neither approach has solved the mystery, though "Bigfooters" still heatedly debate both sides.[12]

For nearly half a century, until his death in 2001, Dr. Bernard Heuvelmans persistently maintained that "there are lost worlds everywhere," in which new species may be found by those who care to look. "The great days of zoology," he cheerfully insisted, "are not done."[13] Most mainstream scientists today stop short of sharing Baron Cuvier's contempt for new discoveries, but few of them grant that a lake "monster" or Skunk Ape falls within the realm of credibility. Perhaps the evidence to prove them wrong awaits discovery in Florida—should anyone take time to seek it out.

Appendix

Florida Skunk Ape Encounters

The following timeline presents abbreviated information on all Skunk Ape sightings reported since 1818. Undated reports are found at the end of the list. Sources from the bibliography are identified by the following abbreviations:

BAA	Rife, *Bigfoot across America*
BF	Coleman, *Bigfoot!*
BFC	Bord and Bord, *Bigfoot Casebook*
BFE	Bigfoot Encounters
BFRO	Bigfoot Field Researchers Organization
BOEC	Berry, *Bigfoot on the East Coast*
CGMB	Keel, *Complete Guide to Mysterious Beings*
CZ	Cryptozoology
GCBRO	Gulf Coast Bigfoot Research Organization
MA	Coleman, *Mysterious America*
MC	Eberhart, *Mysterious Creatures*
NDN	*Naples Daily News*
OS	*Orlando Sentinel*
OSS	*Orlando Sentinel Star*
STAAU	Green, *Sasquatch: The Apes among Us*
TD	*Tallahassee Democrat*
UX20	Bord and Bord, *Unexplained Mysteries of the 20th Century*

Information listed includes date, witness, location, brief description, and source(s).

July 1818
unnamed
Apalachicola
5-foot "baboon" reported, traced to "nest" at cotton warehouse.
Apalachicola Gazette via *Edinburgh Advertiser* (21 July 1818)

July 1872
unnamed
San Pedro Bay
Hairy "wild man" seen in and around local swamp.
Augusta (Maine) Daily Kennebec Journal (12 July 1872)

September 1900
Mrs. Arthur Shiver, Bill Went and others
Kissimmee
"Wild man" seen and pursued repeatedly.
Davenport (Iowa) Daily Leader (28 September 1900)

1942
"Isaac"
south of Branford
Hairy manlike creature hopped on running board of car, riding for half a mile.
BFE; BOEC, 77

1947
4-year-old boy
Lakeland
Child saw a large primate outside his home.
BFC, 160; BOEC, 77; STAAU, 271; UX20, 362

Summer 1947 or 1948
teen girl
near Palatka
"Large dark figure" scratching back on tree.
BFRO #4795

1957
unnamed
Everglades
unknown
CZ

Spring 1957
"W. D." and 2 friends
Big Cypress Swamp

Large primate with glowing eyes roused hunters from sleep, staring at them for 2 minutes.
BFC, 162; BOEC, 77; STAAU, 271–72; UX20, 362; message posted to Chupacabra@yahoogroups.com (6 Dec. 2005)

Late 1950s
Doug Tarrant
unknown
Witness claims "three experiences of encounters," sans details.
ForestGiants@yahoogroups.com (13 Jan. 2006)

1958 or 1959
unnamed
Highway 46, Seminole Co.
unknown
CZ

1959
unnamed
Wekiva River
unknown
CZ

1959
unnamed
Apopka
unknown
CZ

1960s
unnamed
Bull Bay, near Cayo Pelau
Fisherman reports Skunk Ape "families" wading between islands.
BOEC, 77

1960s
unnamed
unknown
Man told the FWCC that he lived with a Skunk Ape family for 6 months.
NDN (22 Sept. 2005)

1960s
Doug Tarrant
unknown
Witness in canoe reported two separate sightings of primates 7 feet tall and 400 pounds.
ForestGiants@yahoogroups.com (13 Feb. 2006)

15 Aug. 1962
Boy Scouts
Quednau Ranch, Charlotte Co.
Shrieking bipedal creature.
BFRO #445

Winter 1962
unnamed
Hialeah
"Hairy thing" eating guavas.
BFE

1963
several unnamed
Holopaw
Residents saw an apelike creature run across a field.
BFC, 168; BFE; BOEC, 77; CGMB, 109; UX20, 362

Spring 1963
9-year-old boy
North Ft. Myers
Bipedal creature "taller than a man," seen after "several" sightings by others in preceding weeks.
BFRO #6692

Mid-1960s
unnamed
near Brooksville
Youth changing flat tire saw an apelike creature watching.
BOEC, 77

1966
unnamed
Apopka
unknown
CZ

1966
unnamed
Osceola Co.
Farmhand fled after a large primate approached his truck and peered through a window, growling.
BAA, 61–62

Spring 1966
Eula Lewis
Brooksville

Large primate chased woman into her home, flailing arms at dogs.
BFC, 171; BOEC, 77; UX20, 362

Summer 1966
Ralph Chambers
near Elfers
Witness saw a primate 7 feet tall and 4 feet wide, exuding "rancid, putrid odor." Dogs refused to track it. Chambers later reported a second sighting of the same animal.
BFC, 172; BOEC, 77; MC, 392; UX20, 362

Nov. 1966
Eugene Crosby
Holopaw
5-foot-tall primate threw a tire tube at the witness on Deseret Farms, returning three times the same night to open a gate.
BOEC, 78; CGMB, 109; OS (1 April 2005)

Nov. 1966
2 unnamed
Holopaw
Hunters on Deseret Farms fired at a 6-foot primate that "attacked" them.
CGMB, 109

30 Nov. 1966
"Miss M. B."
Brooksville
While changing flat tire at 10 p.m., witness saw a 7-foot creature with green eyes 2 inches in diameter watching her.
BAA, 62; BFC, 173; BOEC, 78; CGMB, 110; STAAU, 272; UX20, 362

Dec. 1966
2 unnamed
Anclote River
Hunters saw a large unknown primate.
BFC, 173; BOEC, 78; UX20, 362

1967
unnamed
Brooksville
unknown
CZ

Jan. 1967
4 unnamed
Elfers
Teenagers reported primate the size of a chimp, with foul odor and glowing green eyes, leaping onto hood of their car.
BFC, 173–74; BOEC, 78

Early 1967
Ralph Chambers
near Elfers
Witness saw a 7-foot primate emerge from swamp.
BOEC, 78; UX20, 362

Summer 1967
Ralph Chambers
Elfers
Witness watched his dogs chase a large primate from his yard into nearby swamp.
BFC, 174; BOEC, 78

9 July 1967
"James P."
near Brooksville
8-foot primate grabbed trucker sleeping in his cab, then fled when witness hit his horn.
BOEC, 78

1969
Henry Ring
near Davie
Witness saw a large primate treed by dogs in an orange grove. It escaped by swinging through trees and diving into a canal.
BFC, 183; BOEC, 78; UX20, 362

1969
Charles Robertson
near Davie
Hunter met growling, smelly primate in a guava orchard.
BFC, 182–83; BOEC, 78

1969
Robert Goble
near Ft. Pierce
Motorist saw an 8-foot primate grubbing for roots in swamp. It left 18-inch footprints with a 4-foot stride.
BOEC, 79

1969
"Leon C."
near Brooksville
Motorist on State Rd. 50 reported that a large primate "smacked" and pursued his car.
BOEC, 79

1969–72
teenagers

around "the Rock Crusher," Citrus Co.
Multiple nocturnal sightings by "partying" teens.
GCBRO

1969–80
"L. W."
Hernando Co., between Brooksville and Spring Hill
Multiple footprint discoveries and one sighting of "a being" sitting on wood-
pile; "old timers" claim "several creatures" seen in preceding years.
BFRO #723

1970
unnamed
"Ft. Geneva"
unknown
CZ

1970
unnamed
Gulf of Mexico
Fisherman from Placida claimed sighting of a primate swimming 20 miles
offshore.
BOEC, 79

1970
unnamed
Apopka
unknown
CZ

1970
unnamed
Mims
unknown
CZ

1970
unnamed
north of Brooksville
Truck driver sleeping in his cab attacked by primate. It fled when he cried
out, attracting dogs.
BOEC, 79. [Virtual duplicate of 9 July 1967 incident]

Feb. 1970 or 1971
H. C. Osborn and others
Big Cypress Swamp?
Archaeologists woke when a large, foul-smelling primate invaded their camp,
leaving 17½-inch tracks.
BAA, 64–65; BFC, 184, 187; BOEC, 79; MC, 505; STAAU, 272–73; UX20, 362.

Early 1970s
2 unnamed
Peace River City
Boys saw an apelike creature emerge from riverside cave, swim across the river, and walk into woods on the other side.
BOEC, 79

Early 1970s .
2 unnamed
Cross Bayou Canal, Pinellas Park
Hunters followed 18-inch footprints into swamp, meeting huge, malodorous primate.
BOEC, 79

1971
unnamed
Apopka
unknown
CZ

1971
unnamed
Brooksville
Woman hanging clothes on line behind house met a large primate.
BOEC, 79

1971
unnamed
Broward Co.
Witness reported two Skunk Apes walking together. The larger was gray, with numerous "splotches" and sores; the smaller was dark brown or black.
MA, 210

1971
Harry Rose, Joseph Simbili
near Davie
Witnesses saw a huge primate while guarding a mobile home against prowlers. The beast left 14-inch tracks.
BOEC, 79; UX20, 362

April 1971
L. Frank Hudson
near St. Petersburg
Witness followed tracks through swamp and met a Skunk Ape.
BOEC, 79

Summer 1971 or 1972
2 unnamed
Putnam Hall, Putnam Co.

"Savage" figure with "cave man type face" and "dirty torn clothes" glimpsed beside highway in fog, at 2 a.m.
BFRO #1719; GCBRO

6 July 1971
Ray Fairman
south of Belle Glade
Trucker stopped for "hitchhiker," then fled on foot when an 8-foot primate smelling like rotten flesh climbed into his cab.
BAA, 64; BOEC, 79

Aug. 1971
Henry Ring
west of Ft. Lauderdale
Rabies control officer saw large primate cross the highway during search sparked by "many reports."
BF, 162; BFC, 188; BOEC, 80; MA, 216; STAAU, 273

1971–76
unnamed
Dunnellon
Resident claimed a five-year series of Skunk Ape sightings on his property, including discovery of 3-toed footprints.
BOEC, 87

1972
unnamed
Crystal River
Man shot a hairy biped that escaped into a swamp.
BOEC, 79

1972
"Duane H."
north of Pinellas Park
Farmer's cow killed and truck damaged by unseen prowler who left "huge" footprints.
BFE; BOEC, 81

1972
unnamed
near Davie
Farmer found a 300-pound bull "torn apart," with 3-toed 18-inch footprints nearby.
BOEC, 81

March 1972
unnamed
"Bull Key"
Fisherman reported Skunk Ape "families" wading between islands in "Coya Pelau" area; apparent reference to Cayo Pelau near Bull Bay.
BFE; *St. Petersburg Times-Floridian* (26 March 1972). [Duplicates previous 1960s report above]

May 1972
Allen Carter and siblings
Brooksville
Several children saw a 7-foot primate with a "baby" in the family's yard, apparently eating roots.
BOEC, 79

15 May 1972
2 boys
near Youngstown
Nocturnal sighting of hairy gray figure walking through tall grass near campsite.
BFRO #5519

15 June 1972
2 unnamed
35 miles from Silver Springs, Putnam Co.
Nocturnal roadside sighting of primate with long reddish hair, 3–4 feet tall.
GCBRO

1973
David and Jack Shealy
Everglades, Collier Co.
Hunters glimpsed large primate.
NDN (22 Sept. 2005)

1973
"Duane H."
north of Pinellas Park
Farmer reported more cattle killed by large unseen creature.
BFE

1973
"Don"
Stark Co.
Large primate seen, no further details available.
BFE

1973
2 unnamed

near Punta Gorda
Large primate with green eyes and skunklike odor emerged from fog to stare in car windows.
BOEC, 81

1973
"Richard W." and friends
west of Brooksville
Primate 7–8 feet tall interrupted a cookout, then fled into woods.
BOEC, 81–82

Feb. 1973
"Mason O."
near Brooksville
Witness saw a large primate on the Kelly farm, north of Highway 476, where "animal deaths" were reported.
BOEC, 81

May 1973
2 unnamed
Collier Co.
Creature 8–9 feet tall with long, "whispy" hair frightened campers at night.
BFRO #2856

July 1973
Terrance Craigsmith and father
Immokalee
Primate 7–8 feet tall jumped over the witnesses' truck and fled into swamp. Police cast 15-inch footprints.
BOEC, 81

23 Aug. 1973
4 or 5 children
Twin Lakes Estates, Ft. Myers
Brown or gray "something" seen in woods near playground.
BFRO #1030

24 Oct. 1973
Michael Polesnek
near Hollywood
Farmer reports attack on livestock by something that left 14-inch 3-toed footprints.
BOEC, 81

25 Oct. 1973
"Danny L." and 7 friends
Broward Co.
Teenagers saw a 7-foot biped on the porch of an unfinished building.
BOEC, 81

Nov. 1973
"Debbie and Nancy K."
near Brooksville
Motorists saw a large primate cross Highway 476 near the Kelly farm.
BOEC, 81

Late 1973
unnamed
"Hollywood" (actually Hialeah)
Trucker changing a flat tire 6 miles west of Highways 27 and 41 saw a large
primate approaching. Police found footprints.
BOEC, 82

1974
3 teens
Pasco Co.
Screams and heavy-breathing sounds frightened adolescents on a rural
lovers' lane.
GCBRO

1974
3 unnamed
near Brooksville
Girls encountered a large apelike creature near Highway 50.
BOEC, 84

9 Jan. 1974
Robert Hollymeal
Ft. Lauderdale
Policeman shot a hairy biped, which escaped.
BOEC, 82; UX20, 362

9 Jan. 1974
Terrance Craigsmith
Immokalee
Large primate killed a pony, then jumped fence when rancher fired shots.
BOEC, 82

9 Jan. 1974
Richard Lee Smith
Dade Co.
Motorist reported striking a 7-foot primate on State Rd. 27, at 3:30 a.m. Two
hours later, second motorist reported the creature limping along roadside 5
miles away.
BOEC, 82

Feb. 1974
Mrs. George Kelly and daughter
north of Brooksville

Large primate sighted on farm.
BFE

1 March 1974
unnamed
north of Brooksville
Nocturnal sighting of a Skunk Ape near a trash pile on the Kelly farm.
BOEC, 82

11 March 1974
Duane and Ramona Hibner
north of Brooksville
Motorists saw three "man-monkey" creatures eating from roadside trash pile
near the Kelly farm.
BOEC, 82

April 1974
2 unnamed
near Brooksville
Workers at Seven Hills Nursery, off Highway 98, observed two 7-foot primates.
BOEC, 82

April 1974
Duane Hibner
north of Brooksville
Witness saw an 8-foot biped on Highway 476, near the Kelly farm.
BOEC, 82

Early June 1974
Victor Robinson and friend
White Horse Key, Ten Thousand Islands
Fishermen found 18-inch footprints with 4½-foot stride on beach at mid-
night.
BFE; BOEC, 83

July 1974
3 young boys
Inverness
"Large hairy man" seen in woods outside town.
GCBRO

15 July 1974
5 unnamed
Everglades, west of Lake Worth
Primate "family" seen, including 12-foot "dad," "mom" 8–10 feet tall, and
7-foot "young one." Primary witness claims subsequent yearlong series of
sightings on same property.
BFRO #414

29 July 1974
Conrad and Nancy Paisley, with friends
Croom Wildlife Preserve, Withlacoochee State Forest
Campers saw a 7-foot primate, making sounds "like a goat."
BOEC, 83

Sept. 1974
"Mr. and Mrs. Taylor"
near Brooksville
Residents saw a 3-foot-tall primate in their backyard, off Highway 98. It
made sounds like a baby crying.
BOEC, 83

24 Sept. 1974
unnamed
near Palm Beach
Security guard at unfinished housing development fired six shots at a 7-foot
primate that smelled like rotten eggs. The creature grabbed its chest and
fled.
BAA, 65–66; BFC, 201; BOEC, 83; UX20, 362

Late Sept. 1974
"Elaine R." and cousin
near Brooksville
Motorists reported seeing a shaggy, foul-smelling primate beside a dirt road
off Highway 50.
BOEC, 83

Oct. 1974
unnamed woman
Florida Turnpike
Driver struck large primate with car.
BFE

Oct. 1974
unnamed
near Brooksville
Woman reported a Skunk Ape limping through her yard on Colorado Rd.
BOEC, 83

Oct. 1974
several unnamed
east of Ft. Myers
Motorists report a Skunk Ape following their car.
BOEC, 83–84

Mid-Oct. 1974
2 unnamed

near Brooksville
Women reported seeing huge primate sitting in the middle of a rural road. Sheriff found humanoid footprints. One witness claimed previous incidents of strange vocalizations and banging on her trailer.
BOEC, 83

Nov. 1974
several hunters
Corkscrew Swamp, Collier Co.
8-foot creature with reddish brown hair and foul odor seen at midnight.
GCBRO

19 Dec. 1974
2 unnamed
Weeki Watchee River
Hikers saw a 7-foot, glossy-black primate on the riverbank.
BOEC, 84

1975
unnamed
Alachua Co.
unknown
CZ

1975
unnamed
Everglades
"Several reports."
CZ

1975
unnamed
near Venice
Nocturnal sighting of a hairy biped on Havana Rd., near Blackburn Canal.
BOEC, 86

1975
2 unnamed
near Venice
Boys told sheriff they were chased by a tall primate while riding bicycles.
BOEC, 86

1975
several unnamed
near Venice
Workmen pouring concrete glimpsed and pursued a tall bipedal creature.
BOEC, 86

1975
unnamed
Polk Co.
Motorist claimed he struck a large primate carrying an armload of corn.
BOEC, 87

1975
unnamed
Polk Co.
Woman saw a primate with long flowing hair, running "faster than a horse."
BOEC, 87

1975
unnamed
Polk Co.
15-inch humanoid footprints found in an orange grove near Green Swamp.
BOEC, 87

1975
2 unnamed
near Laurel
Hairy biped frightened two girls from their rural campsite.
BOEC, 87

1975
unnamed
Moon Lake, near Port Richey
"Several reports."
CZ

Jan. 1975
unnamed
Pasco Co.
Predawn sighting of an amber-eyed primate, howling and whistling on a dairy farm.
BOEC, 84

Jan. 1975
unnamed
near Miami
Motorist on the Florida Turnpike struck a large primate, then stopped her car and saw it standing at roadside.
BOEC, 84

15 Jan. 1975
2 boys
Coral Springs, between Sample Rd. and Wiles Rd.
"Large, black-brown human-like form" seen in shrubbery.
BFRO #592

Mid-Jan. 1975
Allen Goding
Florida City
12-inch footprints found at Homestead Fisheries.
BOEC, 84

23 Jan. 1975
Kim Dunn
Miramar
Rookie policeman saw large primate cross a road.
BFC, 203; BOEC, 84; UX20, 362

Late Jan. 1975
Richard Taylor
Pasco Co.
Second sighting on local dairy farm. Primate limped and seemed to have a broken arm.
BOEC, 84

Feb. 1975
Steve Voreh
south of Gainesville
Motorist struck an 8-foot primate on Williston Rd., then shot it before it fled.
BOEC, 85

2 Feb. 1975
Richard Davis
Cape Coral
Witness fired one shot at a 9-foot hairy primate.
BFC, 121, 203; BOEC, 84; UX20, 362

3 Feb. 1975
Richard Davis
Cape Coral
Witness shot the same creature outside his rural home, but it escaped.
BOEC, 84–85

12 Feb. 1975
Suzanne Thompson
Live Oak
Nocturnal sighting of a hairy biped at 50 yards, under lights.
BOEC, 85

March 1975
"Mrs. Morrison"
near Brooksville
Witness saw a 6-foot primate eating oranges, snapping thick branches from

the tree. She claimed previous sightings, nocturnal screams, and slaughter of various farm animals.
BOEC, 85

6 March 1975
Steve Humphreys and wife
near Lake Okeechobee
Motorists struck "huge" primate on highway at 11:20 p.m., badly denting their car. Hair samples collected for analysis (result unknown).
BFC, 203; BOEC, 85; UX20, 362

14 March 1975
unnamed
near Brooksville
Motorist saw a hairy biped cross Highway 41 at 8:30 p.m.
BOEC, 85

24 March 1975
Michael Bennett and Lawrence Groom
Black Point, Dade Co.
Witnesses saw a primate 8–9 feet tall rocking a truck as its driver fled on foot. Their headlights frightened the creature away.
BAA, 66; BFC, 121, 203; BOEC, 84; UX20, 362

May 1975
4 children
West Palm Beach
Witnesses reported a huge apelike creature.
BOEC, 86

5 or 7 June 1975
Ronnie Steves
Venice
12-year-old boy claimed two sightings of a 6-foot black primate in one day, first chasing ducks, then pushing down a chain-link fence.
BFC, 204; BOEC, 87; MC, 505; STAAU, 276–78; UX20, 362

July 1975
3 unnamed
near Brooksville
Daylight sighting of a 7-foot primate standing in a ditch beside Highway 581.
BOEC, 86

21 July 1975
unnamed
Brooksville
Motorist saw a "hairy man" cross Highway 41 North at dusk.
BOEC, 86

25 July 1975
2 unnamed
Brooksville
Men walking along Highway 581 at 1 a.m. report being followed by an unseen, foul-smelling creature in woods.
BOEC, 86

Aug. 1975
unnamed
near Brooksville
Farmer mowing his pasture at dusk reported a large primate watching him.
BOEC, 86

14 Aug. 1975
"Mrs. John M." and 3 sons
North Ft. Myers
Witnesses reported being chased by a Skunk Ape 4½–5 feet tall. One child claimed he saw it eat a bird.
BOEC, 86; STAAU, 278; UX20, 362

Nov. 1975
John Sohl and others
northeast of Homosassa Springs, Citrus Co.
Witnesses saw 3 primates, ranging in height from 5 to 8 feet. Sohl returned later with a camera and met one creature, which tossed him 15 feet after he snapped a photo.
BFC, 122, 206–7; BOEC, 86; UX20, 362

Late 1975
Joyce Hudson's step-brother
near Brooksville
Witness saw an 8-foot primate jump the bank on Croom Rd. and enter an orange grove.
BOEC, 87

1975–79
several unnamed
rural Manatee Co.
Reporting witness claims multiple sightings of primate 5–9 feet tall, accompanied by shrieking sounds.
GCBRO

17 Jan. 1976
2 unnamed
unknown
Hairy biped frightened girls from their campsite.
BOEC, 87. [Possible duplicate of 1975 Laurel incident]

29 Feb. 1976
unnamed
Dunnellon
Hiker found 18-inch 4-toed footprints and other evidence of a large creature's passage along the Withlacoochee River
BOEC, 87

April 1976
unnamed
Lake Lindsay, near Brooksville
Woman saw a large primate cross a pasture at sunrise.
BOEC, 87

6 June 1976
Bill and John Holley, John Kensey
Ft. Myers
Nocturnal sighting of a large primate with long black hair beside Route 31. Sheriff's deputy found footprints 2–3 inches deep.
BFC, 209; BOEC, 88

15 June 1976
Tom Williams
Grove City
Nocturnal spotlight sighting of a primate 4–5 feet tall, drinking from pond.
BOEC, 88

17 June 1976
Michael Bridges and 13 others
Conservation Area No. 3, Everglades
Passengers on tour boat saw 7-foot, 500-pound primate at close range.
BOEC, 88

Mid-June 1976
3 unnamed
Grove City
Youths report seeing a Skunk Ape with long reddish brown hair twice in one night.
BFC, 209; BOEC, 87

25 June 1976
several unnamed
Croom Wildlife Preserve, 17 miles west of Brooksville
Campers reported an 8-foot primate that smelled "like a dead animal."
BOEC, 88

Summer 1976
3 unnamed
near Brooksville

Children saw a hairy biped walking in a drainage ditch at dusk.
BOEC, 88

Summer 1976
unnamed
Brooksville
"Many sightings of Bigfoot."
BFC, 211; UX20, 362

July 1976
Martha Cowell and friend
Port Orange
Primate 7–7½ feet tall, covered with "Irish-setter red-colored hair," seen
beside Taylor Rd. at 2 a.m.
BFE

July 1976
unnamed
near Brooksville
Man reported seeing a tall apelike creature.
BOEC, 88

17–18 July 1976
Donald Duncan and son
Dunnellon
Man and child reported sightings of a Skunk Ape fighting with their dogs,
one of which was killed. After gunshots, the beast ran into nearby woods
"howling like a wolf."
BOEC, 88

15 Aug. 1976
2 girls, age 9 and 5
Esto, Holmes Co.
"Huge" biped with brownish red hair seen in woods, "definitely not a bear."
BFRO #115

Sept. 1976
MacDonald children
Ft. Myers
Several witnesses saw a primate standing in a clump of trees.
BOEC, 89

24 Oct. 1976
"Joseph"
south of Orlando
15-year-old boy claimed a primate 9–10 feet tall attacked him in woods at
12:10 a.m.
BOEC, 89

1977
unnamed
Apopka
unknown
CZ

1977
Mike Corradino
Venice
Witness found 17-inch footprints "in a human pattern."
BOEC, 92

1977
unnamed
Gibsonton
17-inch footprints discovered.
BFE

1977
unnamed
Marion Co.
unknown
BFE

Jan. 1977
"Percy"
Moon Lake
Witness reported a "very large" hairy biped.
BOEC, 89

Feb. 1977
several unnamed
Ft. Myers
ROTC members searched woods after a reported Skunk Ape sighting, discovering humanoid footprints "16 × 18 inches."
BOEC, 89

Early Feb. 1977
unnamed
Delray Beach
Golf course manager saw a 7-foot shaggy primate drinking from a lake.
BFC, 212; BOEC, 89

Early Feb. 1977
unnamed
Delray Beach
Security guard saw an apelike biped on golf course.
BFC, 213; BOEC, 89; UX20, 362

Early Feb. 1977
unnamed
Delray Beach
Motorist told police of seeing a large primate cross a rural road.
BOEC, 89

16 Feb. 1977
Charles Noreen and Jay Wilson
Moon Lake
Witnesses saw 3 creatures with "faces like gorillas," the largest 10 feet tall.
The animals left 18-inch footprints.
BFC, 213; BOEC, 89; STAAU, 280; UX20, 362

Spring 1977
Chip Coffey
Oneco
Motorist reports two sightings of a large primate along State Rd. 70, two
weeks apart.
BOEC, 89

25 March 1977
Bob Saver and David Smith
Delray Beach
Motorcyclists saw a 10-foot primate walking down the middle of a rural
road.
BOEC, 90; STAAU, 280

2 April 1977
Dick, Ray, and Jerry Williams
Moon Lake
Driver and passengers saw a 9-foot biped cross the road at 9:15 p.m.
BOEC, 90; STAAU, 280; UX20, 362

8 April 1977
Charles Wilson
Moon Lake
"Huge" primate pounded on the witness's trailer then fled, leaving 22-inch
footprints.
BOEC, 90; STAAU, 280

13 May 1977
Terrance Craigsmith and Robert Merritt
Nobleton
Dogs pursued and fought a large primate that left 13-inch footprints.
BFC, 214; BOEC, 90; UX20, 362

14 May 1977
unnamed
Nobleton

Man claims he saw a 6-foot primate, gray with red eyes, trying to enter his tool shed. It left 13-inch footprints.
BOEC, 90

23 May 1977
Tony Collins, Bobby McCoy, Willie James Silvers, Bobby Lee Turner
10 miles south of Labelle
After their car died on State Rd. 29, witnesses saw a large primate cross the road in 3 strides.
BFC, 214; BOEC, 90; STAAU, 280; UX20, 362

14 July 1977
Charlie Stoeckman and son
north of Tavernier
Bottle-hunters smelled an odor like "wet dog," then saw a "huge" primate that made sounds "like a dolphin bark."
BFC, 215; BOEC, 90

21 July 1977
2 unnamed
Key Largo
Men saw a large primate standing in a field.
BFC, 215; BOEC, 91; UX20, 362

22 July 1977
Leslie Stoeckman
north of Tavernier
Witness saw primate "towering" over 8-foot-tall brush at 3 a.m.
BOEC, 91

Aug. 1977
3 unnamed
Oneco
Teenagers saw a hairy "unclothed" primate running along a road.
BOEC, 91

1 Aug. 1977
Tony Dault, Frank Luke, Grant Prince
Bradenton
Card players smelled foul odor, then saw a creature with glowing eyes that ran "like a hunchback."
BOEC, 91

15 Aug. 1977
Darlene MacDonald's son
Captiva Island
Boy saw a tall, hairy primate with a "crab-like" walk that left "indistinct" tracks.
BOEC, 91

2 Sept. 1977
Sean MacDonald
Captiva Island
Child saw a primate walking on all fours, then upright.
BOEC, 91. [Virtual duplicate of 15 Aug. 1977 incident]

2 Oct. 1977
unnamed
south of Belleview
Hitchhiker claimed he was attacked by a foul-smelling 6-foot primate along
U.S. Highway 441.
BFC, 218; BOEC, 91; OSS (5 Oct. 1977); UX20, 362

3 Oct. 1977
Donnie Hall
Apopka
Security guard at John's Nursery shot a 10-foot primate that ripped off his
shirt. FWCC agent found tracks that "appeared to be manmade."
BFC, 218; BOEC, 91; OSS (5 Oct. 1977); UX20, 362

11 Oct. 1977
Rev. S. L. Whatley
near Ft. McCoy, Ocala National Forest
While cutting wood at 2 p.m., the witness saw a primate 7–8 feet tall.
BAA, 66; BFC, 131–32, 218; BOEC, 91–92; OSS (16 Nov. 1977); *Superior (Wisc.)*
Evening Telegram (15 Nov. 1977); UX20, 362

Autumn 1977
John Allen and mother
Oneco
Witnesses saw a "hunched-over" primate walking beside a road.
BOEC, 92

18 Nov. 1977
unnamed
Big Scrub Campsites, Ocala National Forest
Hunter fired 6 shots at an 800-pound apelike creature.
BOEC, 92; OSS (19 Nov. 1977)

1978
unnamed
Ocala National Forest
unknown
CZ

1978
unnamed
west of Winter Haven
Nocturnal sighting of an 8-foot "hairy man" by moonlight.
BOEC, 92

Early 1978
multiple unnamed
"southwest coast"
Busload of tourists en route to the Everglades saw a 9-foot primate walking upright.
BOEC, 92

March 1978
multiple unnamed
near Jay
Five truckloads of men fled a brownish black primate 6½–8 feet tall, with long arms and a strong smell.
BOEC, 92

April 1978
unnamed
Manatee Co.
Woman roused from home by a foul smell and "inhuman howling" found 20-inch footprints.
BOEC, 92

5 April 1978
Chip Coffey
Oneco
Witness found 23-inch humanoid footprints in his backyard.
BOEC, 92

June 1978
2 young children
Hudson
8-foot "dark figure" seen near mobile home on two separate nights, leaving footprints and "fist print" in aluminum siding on second visit.
BFRO #7627

July 1978
teenage boy
Jonathan Dickinson State Park
"Something" 6–7 feet tall, covered with shaggy silver-gray hair, seen in woods at night.
BFRO #5369

Aug. 1978
8 children
Flagler Beach
Daylight sighting of a 7-foot biped covered with long brownish gray hair.
BFRO #2657

Dec. 1978 or Jan. 1979
2 young children
Hudson
"Dark figure" seen in shrubbery near bus stop, by same witnesses from June 1978 encounters.
BFRO #7627

1979
unnamed
Ocala National Forest
unknown
CZ

5 Feb. 1979
4 unnamed
near Jacksonville
Travelers stranded on Interstate 95 saw a white 8-foot primate that passed through underbrush "like a tank."
BOEC, 92

Aug. 1979
several carpenters
Ochopee
Workers saw "tall, hairy creature" emerge from basement of rural house undergoing demolition, noting its foul odor and reddish brown hair.
BFRO #7205

Summer 1979 or 1980
3 unnamed
east of Lakeland, Polk Co.
"Unusual animal noises heard at night" on several occasions, accompanied by knocking sounds from woods.
BFRO #1608

Early 1980s
2 unnamed
North Port, near Myakka State Forest
Child complained of "something" peering in his window at night. Father found breath condensation on window pane and saw a "very large," malodorous biped flee the property.
BFRO #8561

1980s
unnamed
Canaveral Groves
"Several reports."
CZ

1980
unnamed
Paisley
unknown
CZ

1980
unnamed
Lake Co.
unknown
BFE

1980
unnamed
Broward Co.
unknown
BFE

Spring 1980
unnamed woman
Orange Co., 20 miles outside Orlando
"Bigfoot" attacked mobile home, tearing door off hinges.
BFRO #1275

May 1980
unnamed
near Eustis
Motorist saw a tall hairy biped cross the highway.
BOEC, 93

June 1980
unnamed
Ocala National Forest
Contractor working near Camp Ocala found 17-inch footprints with a 4-foot stride.
BOEC, 93

12 June 1980
Jim Spink
near mouth of the Peace River, Charlotte Co.
Witness allegedly photographed a Skunk Ape.
BOEC, 93

30 June 1980
several
northwest of Alexander Springs, Lake Co.
"Many large footprints" found, several cast in plaster. Sheriff's spokesman called the incident a hoax.
BFRO #5510; GCBRO; *Houston Chronicle* (2 July 1980)

15 July 1980
3 boys
Davie
"Something" waved its arms at the boys from across a canal.
BFRO #594

1981 or 1982
S. LePage and cousins
Near Holopaw
Howling cries accompanied by foul odor.
Bigfoot@yahoogroups.com (22 November 2005)

7 Aug. 1981
3 boys, age 10–12
Sarasota
7-foot "human like figure" seen in wooded area of Acorn Circle neighbor-hood.
BFRO #10867

15 Aug. 1981
2 boys
Inglis
Children frightened by howling sounds "exactly the same" as alleged Bigfoot recordings from Ohio.
BFRO #430

Oct. 1981
2 children
Casselberry
Crashing sounds in woods frightened children on their way to school; searchers found a large branch freshly torn from tree. One child's mother heard similar sounds a few nights later.
BFRO #1079

1982
Randy Medlock
near Baird
Motorist saw a large pug-nosed biped cross the highway, leaving footprints larger than the witness's size-13 shoes.
BOEC, 93

Jan. 1982
14-year-old boy
near Milton, Santa Rosa Co.
Witness saw "a large reddish brown unknown animal" running on its hind legs.
BFRO #989

1983
unnamed
Citrus Co.
unknown
BFE

16 July 1983
father and son
Citrus Wildlife Management Area, north of Brooksville
Nocturnal hunters met creature 7–8 feet tall, with eyes "at least 1 foot apart."
BFRO #595

Sept. 1983
11-year-old boy
Geneva
7-foot creature with glowing eyes frightened child at 2 a.m., dented side of trailer.
GCBRO

Nov. 1983
Dan Jackson
Corkscrew Swamp, near Naples
While hunting, smelled an odor like rotten eggs, then saw a creature 6–7 feet tall, weighing 350–400 pounds.
BFE; BFRO #607

June 1984
9-year-old boy
Ruskin
"Large animal" emitting a "God awful odor" frightened a young camper; his 3 companions slept through the encounter.
BFRO #1061

June 1984
several unnamed
near Crews Lake, Pasco Co.
8-foot creature fled hunters, running swiftly into swamp while making "howling/moaning" sounds.
BFRO #737

15 October 1984
2 women
outside St. Augustine
Horseback riders meet a "slim" creature covered in reddish brown hair, described as 6½ feet tall and 250 pounds.
BAA; BFE; BFRO #1003; GCBRO

1984–85
multiple unnamed

Baird
Residents reported "several" sightings of large apelike creatures.
BOEC, 93

1985
several unnamed
Hernando Co.
Residents saw a bipedal primate 7–8 feet tall.
BOEC, 93

Sept. 1985 or 1986
unnamed
near Lakeland
Nocturnal hunter heard "loud blowing noise," then got "a quick glance" at
"something big, loud and smelly," resembling an ape. Subsequently, several
dogs were killed by some unidentified animal.
BFRO #3918

Autumn 1985
"M. R."
Alachua Co.
Psychologist saw an apelike creature covered in leaves or palm fronds cross a
small bridge.
BFRO #2566

1986
unnamed woman
Green Cove Springs, Clay Co.
Motorist saw "somewhat skinny" 6-foot primate crossing State Rd. 209.
BFRO #606. [Nearly duplicates report from April 1994 below, BFRO #8316]

16 Sept. 1986
2 unnamed
Lithia Springs, Hillsborough Co.
Heavyset creature 7–8 feet tall frightened campers at night.
GCBRO

1987
unnamed
Bardin
unknown
CZ

1988 or 1989
several unnamed
Pasco Co.
Same hunters from June 1984 incident reported strange sounds and a rough
"path" where "something" had walked.
BFRO #737

Winter, late 1980s
unnamed
Whitehurst Lake, Hernando Co.
7-foot "man-like thing" walking with "labored" strides.
BFRO #6708

1989
unnamed
Volusia Co.
unknown
BFE

Spring 1989
"P. S." and friend
Oak Hill
Newspaper deliverymen saw a large "ape-like humanoid" on Maytown Rd. at
3:30 a.m. Both witnesses reported a "sickening" odor "like cabbage."
BFRO #746

15 Sept. 1989
2 girls
Cocoa
Creature 7–8 feet tall frightened the witnesses when they stopped to relieve
themselves along Nova Rd.
BFRO #591

1990s
unnamed
Canaveral Groves
"Several reports."
CZ

1990
3 fishermen
Jackson Co., 3 miles west of Greenwood
While fishing from a boat, observed a creature 7–8 feet tall, with "very large
eyes," on the riverbank.
BFRO #724

1990
unnamed
Mims
unknown
CZ

1991
unknown
Oak Hill

unknown
CZ

1991
several unnamed
New Smyrna Beach
Residents sighted a 7-foot, 300-pound primate that smelled like "rotten eggs, moldy cheese and dung."
Daytona Beach News Journal (5 Oct. 2003)

June 1991
"Mr. S" and companions
Levy Co., between Bronson and Williston
Driver and passengers in car see an 8-foot hairy primate cross Highway 27, carrying "a small Bigfoot child" in its arms.
BFRO #1407

Nov. 1991
2 fishermen
Collier Co.
While fishing from boat, witnesses saw a primate wading chest deep in river. They subsequently verified that the water was 7½ feet deep, making the creature "at least 10 feet tall."
GCBRO

1992
unnamed
Melbourne
unknown
CZ

Feb. 1992
unnamed
Everglades Institute, 40 miles west of Miami
"Scattered footfall noises" followed witness through thick undergrowth around 10 p.m.
BFRO #1283

Autumn 1992
unnamed
Lakewood Ranch
Farmer glimpsed a large primate in his headlights at 3 a.m., beside a canal.
Bradenton Herald (14 Feb. 2001)

Date unknown, pre-1993
2 unnamed
east of Sarasota
Large primate approached girls walking on a dirt road. One girl shot it with

a tear-gas gun, causing it to flee screaming. Searchers found large humanoid tracks.
BOEC, 93

Date unknown, pre-1993
2 unnamed
Weedon's Island
Boys heard noises and smelled a "sulfur" odor in woods, later finding 21-inch footprints.
BFE; BOEC, 93

1993
unnamed
Titusville
unknown
CZ

1993
unnamed
Collier Co.
unknown
BFE

Nov. 1993
Alan Mercier
Econ River, near Orlando
Newspaper deliveryman saw a reddish brown primate 5–6 feet tall, with prominent breasts, cross the highway at 4 a.m.
BFE

20 November 1993
5 policemen
Everglades, Collier Co.
While hunting, witnesses found and videotaped "strange" footprints, some "very large," others child-sized "or possibly deformed."
BFRO #720

1993–94
unnamed
Highway 520, Brevard Co.
unknown
CZ

Spring 1994
2 unnamed
Jacksonville
Husband and wife saw a "muscular but rather skinny" creature, 6½–7½ feet

tall and covered with long reddish brown hair, cross Heckscher Drive, illuminated by their headlights.
BFRO #8514

Spring 1994
unnamed
Broward Co., between Hillsboro and Sample
Hiker in woods frightened by footsteps of unseen follower.
BFRO #1831

April 1994
3 unnamed
near Green Cove Springs, Clay Co.
Driver and two passengers saw primate 6–7 feet tall, covered with brown hair and "somewhat skinny," cross State Rd. 16.
BFRO #8316. [Nearly duplicates report from 1986 above, BFRO #606]

April 1994
unnamed
Escambia River near Ala. border, between bridges for Highway 4 and Highway 89
Fisherman in boat saw brown 6½-foot creature walking upright through shallow water.
BFRO #5801

Autumn 1994
unnamed
Broward Co., between Hillsboro and Sample
Brother of "witness" from Broward Co. spring 1994 incident above frightened by sounds of footsteps in the forest.
BFRO #1831

18 Dec. 1994
unnamed
Gadsden Co., near Ga. border
Deer hunter in an open field saw a brown primate roughly 7 feet tall, with shoulders 4–5 feet wide.
BFRO #246

Jan. 1995
unnamed
New Harmony
Nocturnal deer hunter heard shrieking sounds, later "matched" to recordings of alleged Bigfoot calls played on TV.
GCBRO

1 March 1995
2 unnamed
Osprey

While clearing brush, husband and wife found a patch of flattened grass reeking with a stench like rotting flesh. That night, an unseen shrieking creature crashed through shrubbery outside their home. Next morning, they found a trail 8 feet high and 4 feet wide blazed through the woods, with branches 10 inches thick snapped off at the base.
GCBRO

Summer 1995
several unnamed
Blackwater National Forest, near Milton
Men "out drinking" saw a large "thing" watching their camp after nightfall.
GCBRO

July 1996
unnamed
Suwannee Co.
Nurse returning home from work at 3:10 a.m. saw an unknown creature "jogging" along a rural highway. She estimated its weight at "several hundred pounds."
GCBRO

Oct. 1996
"Mr. J" and girlfriend
Alexander Springs, Ocala National Forest
Campers smelled a foul odor and saw a shadowy figure ransack their coolers at 3 a.m.
BFRO #1480

Autumn 1996
5 unnamed
outskirts of Eglin Air Force Base, Okaloosa Co.
Witnesses fled from a "big, upright" figure causing "a commotion" in the woods.
BFRO #730

1997
unnamed
Highlands Co.
Witness saw an 8-foot primate, "extremely muscular" and covered in dirty brown hair, "jogging like a man" in the woods.
GCBRO

1997
2 unnamed
Ocala National Forest, Marion Co.
Driver and his passenger saw a 7-foot, "very slender" primate step from woods beside a rural highway in daylight.
GCBRO

16 July 1997
Steve Goodbread and tourists
Ochopee
Tour guide and his customers observed a brownish 7-foot primate for 15 minutes, while it shook bushes, seeming annoyed at their presence.
BFRO #721

18 July 1997
Dow Roland and tourists
Ochopee
Second tour group saw a 7-foot creature resembling a gorilla.
BFRO #721

21 July 1997
Jan Brock
Ochopee
Motorist saw a large primate cross road 1,000 feet in front of her car at 7:45 a.m.
BFRO #721; MC, 505

21 July 1997
Vince Doerr
Ochopee
Local fire chief photographed a 7-foot reddish brown creature shortly after Jan Brock's sighting.
BFRO #721; *Knoxville News-Sentinel* (13 Oct. 1997); MC, 505–6

24 July 1997
David Shealy
Ochopee
13½-inch footprints found and cast in plaster near scene of Doerr's sighting.
BFRO #721

25 July 1997
"B. B." and 2 children
Ocala National Forest, Marion Co.
Hikers saw "Bigfoot" drinking from a stream.
BFRO #729

Aug. 1997
James McMullen
Everglades, south of Lake Okeechobee
While tracking cougars, witness met a 7-foot, 500-pound primate and cast its 14-inch footprints.
MC, 506; NDN (20 Nov. 1998)

10 Aug. 1997
unnamed
Everglades, Collier Co.

"At least 8 reports in local press."
CZ

17 Aug. 1997
2 unnamed
Ochopee
Bird-watchers saw an unknown 7-foot creature cross a highway after night-
fall; estimated weight, 300–400 pounds.
BFRO #721

20 Oct. 1997
unnamed
Tamiami Trail, Collier Co.
Motorist saw primate cross the road in front of her car at 9 p.m.
CZ

Autumn 1997
Steve Krause
Collier Co.
Witness saw a 7-foot apelike creature, 600 pounds, run into swamp.
CZ

25 Nov. 1997
unnamed
Collier Co.
"Seven reports between Aug. and Nov."
CZ

Jan. 1998
unnamed
near Howard Creek, Gulf Co.
Motorist spotlighting deer saw "huge" primate (6½–7 feet) with "huge red
eyes."
BFRO #7792

9 Feb. 1998
unnamed
Dixie Co.
Motorist saw primate 5–6 feet tall picking up road kill along rural highway at
5 a.m.
BFRO #722

April 1998
unnamed
Osceola Co.
Motorist stopped to relieve himself along Highway 532, followed "strange"
tracks to the carcass of a dead pig.
GCBRO

8 Sept. 1998
David Shealy
Ochopee
Witness snapped 27 photos of a 7-foot primate at his RV park; also found a set of 4-toed footprints.
BFRO #634; NDN (12 Sept. 1998)

Autumn 1998
2 unnamed
Volusia Co.
Loud screams from woods frightened residents and their dogs at 10 p.m.
BFRO #747

22 Nov. 1998
2 unnamed
Three Lakes Wildlife Management Area, Osceola Co.
Deer hunters saw two primates in swamp; 6½-foot male walked "weird and slightly hunched over," followed by 5½-foot female with prominent breasts.
BFRO #733

Dec. 1998
unnamed
Corkscrew Swamp, Collier Co.
Hiker saw a thin red-haired primate, under 6 feet tall, running swiftly "like a man."
GCBRO

30 Dec. 1998
unnamed
Blackwater National Forest, Santa Rosa Co.
Hunter fled at the approach of a long-armed primate emitting high-pitched sounds. Witness returned the next day to photograph footprints and collect hair samples.
GCBRO

2 Jan. 1999
unnamed
Three Lakes Wildlife Management Area, Osceola Co.
Hunter in tree stand observed fast-walking primate 8–9 feet tall, 400–600 pounds, emitting "zoo" odor.
BFRO #736

1999
"Don"
Stark Co.
Resident heard an unknown creature "howling over a dog barking."
BFE

15 Jan. 1999
unnamed
Swamp Fox Lake, Escambia Co.
Hunter in a stand observed a primate at least 7 feet tall, with a "very musky
. . . horrible" smell.
GCBRO

March 1999
unnamed
near Cocoa
Motorist stopping to relieve himself on Nova Rd. found and photographed
six 13-inch footprints with an average 5-foot stride.
BFRO #731

15 March 1999
2 unnamed
Grand Ridge, Jackson Co.
Farmers found unusual tracks, heard moaning sounds, and smelled odor like
"a cross between urine and a dead animal"; neighbors report losing chickens.
GCBRO

April 1999
2 unnamed
Rainbow Lakes Estates, Dunnellon
Child walking to bus stop at 6:30 a.m. saw a "white colored Bigfoot." One
friend claimed a similar encounter.
GCBRO

21 May 1999
"S. S." and friend
near Holopaw
Hunters met a 7½-foot creature, 350–400 pounds.
BFRO #734

Early summer 1999
2 unnamed
North Port, near Myakka State Forest
Husband and wife wake at 2 a.m. to powerful odor and "wild shrieking" outside house. Prowler left breath condensation on window pane 7 feet above
ground.
BFRO #8561

Aug.–Dec. 1999
unnamed
Collier Co.
"Five more sightings."
CZ

Oct. 1999
2 unnamed
Volusia Co.
Dog owned by same "witnesses" from Autumn 1998 injured in yard at 7 a.m.; veterinarian said it was "hit by something big." Male witness claims several co-workers have related encounters with "something resembling Bigfoot."
BFRO #747

30 Nov. 1999
2 unnamed
near Nocturnal
Nocturnal hikers heard odd sounds in woods and glimpsed a "red eye" 7 feet above the ground, by flashlight.
GCBRO

2000
3 unnamed
Polk Co.
Sister-in-law of witness from 1997 Highlands Co. report (above) and her two children saw a Skunk Ape.
GCBRO

Feb. 2000
unnamed
Jacksonville
Resident of Deerwood Park development heard splash, saw large manlike creature rise from lake behind his house and run into woods.
BFRO #446

8 March 2000
several unnamed
Volusia Co.
Campers saw an eye reflecting firelight in the woods, 6½–7 feet above ground before creature retreated.
BFRO #747

April 2000
unnamed
Everglades, south of Chokoloskee
Camper heard "spine-tingling scream" at midnight.
GCBRO

4 May 2000
2 unnamed
Big Cypress Preserve, St. Lucie Co.
Sleepers woke to grunting sounds outside their home, then saw a primate 7–10 feet tall, with "putrid" smell.
GCBRO

Late spring–Dec. 2000
3 unnamed
Summerfield
Local residents report nocturnal screams on various occasions spanning 6–7
months. Neighbors report more than 100 goats killed by unseen predators.
One dog also found with its liver missing.
GCBRO

June 2000
2 unnamed
near Crestview
Men driving to work at 6:45 a.m. saw a large primate cross the road.
BFRO #9113

July 2000
7-year-old boy
near Lakeland
Child glimpsed "Bigfoot" near his grandmother's home.
BFE

July 2000
David Shealy
Collier Co.
While tracking deer with a borrowed video camera, Shealy taped a 7-foot
Skunk Ape near his RV campsite.
BBC News (21 July 2000); MC, 506

22 Aug. 2000
"M. C.," "S. G.," "M. L.," "H. W."
Jacksonville
Security guards at Deerwood Park saw a black "individual" 7–8 feet tall
prowling around the property.
BFRO #446

Sept. 2000
unnamed
Summerfield
Unseen predator "mangled up" a cat and eight goats.
BFRO #598

1 Sept. 2000
"M. G." and "S. G."
Jacksonville
Deerwood Park security guards saw an 8-foot-tall "well proportioned"
prowler.
BFRO #446

6 Sept. 2000
"M. L." and companion

Jacksonville
Deerwood Park security guard and a trespasser heard a loud 30-second growl.
BFRO #446

10 Sept. 2000
"M. C." and "H. W."
Jacksonville
Deerwood Park security guards saw two pairs of glowing orange eyes in their headlights, 6 feet above the ground.
BFRO #446

15 Sept. 2000
"M. C." and "H. W."
Jacksonville
Security guards found several 12-inch footprints on Limerock Trail, in Deerwood Park.
BFRO #446

30 Sept. 2000
unnamed
Dade City
Witness saw 7 large, "smelly" primates "eating, sleeping and howling" in an orange grove at 12:30 a.m. Many large footprints also observed.
GCBRO

15 Oct. 2000
"L. C." and family
Summerfield
Residents fired gunshots in response to nocturnal shrieks and screams, after tape-recording the sounds.
BFRO #598

28 Oct. 2000
"L. C." and 12 others
Summerfield
Nocturnal shrieks and other sounds from woods disrupted party at same home where cries were recorded on 15 Oct.
BFRO #598

3 Nov. 2000
Dave Sidoti and "L. C."
Summerfield
BFRO investigator Sidoti toured the site of recent disturbances, photographing a possible footprint and an apparently deliberate "stick formation."
BFRO #598

29 December 2000
unnamed

Sarasota
Sheriff's department received anonymous letter and several photos allegedly depicting a Skunk Ape seen near the Myakka River weeks earlier.
BF, 150–57; MC, 506

20 Jan. 2001
3 unnamed
Milton
"Growl-scream" sounds disturbed residents between 8:30 and 11:00 p.m.
GCBRO

25 Feb. 2001
"Don" and friend
Stark Co.
Driver and his passenger saw a large primate cross a rural road at "incredible" speed, around 6 p.m. On 26 Feb. they found a 14-inch footprint at the site.
BFE

March 2001
unnamed
"the Watson Place," near Chokoloskee
Camper frightened by "piercing screams" at 11:30 p.m. Earlier, a ranger warned him of "locals harassing the campers."
BFRO #2915

29 June 2001
2 unnamed
New Smyrna Beach
Husband and wife saw a large "shadowy" figure walking in the surf by moonlight, at 11:30 p.m.
BFRO #2848

4 Oct. 2001
unnamed
outside Tampa
Nocturnal hiker saw a reddish brown primate crouched beside stream, with one hand in water.
GCBRO

26 Nov. 2001
2 unnamed
Sorrento
Residents heard "unexplainable sounds . . . like cries of pain" spanning 10 minutes.
GCBRO

31 Dec. 2001
2 unnamed

east side of Tallahassee
Children saw a "furry" creature with red eyes near Mahan Drive, between
8:30 and 9:00 p.m. It "walked funny," with an apparent limp.
BFRO #5702

15 Jan. 2002
several unnamed
Mary Esther, Okaloosa Co.
"Unexplainable sounds" interrupted a card party. Players glimpsed a "hairy,
dark brown figure" slipping into woods, then found 21-inch footprints and
a handprint "three times" normal size in dirt. "Growling sounds" thereafter
recurred "every once in a while."
GCBRO

12 March 2002
2 unnamed
4 miles outside Destin
Driver and passenger parked beside a rural highway saw a 7-foot, "muscular-
ish" primate in the woods and smelled its "very, very pungent" odor.
GCBRO

Autumn 2002
Patricia Edwards
Green Swamp, near Ocala
Motorist saw a primate cross County Rd. 471, first "galloping" on all fours,
then standing erect.
OS (6 Sept. 2003, 4 Sept. 2005)

2003
2 unnamed
Grassy Waters Preserve, Palm Beach Co.
Visitors saw a "big dark figure" pull something from water and eat it, at 5:30
p.m.
BFRO #7904

Feb. 2003
2 unnamed
Ochopee
David Shealy reported that a Skunk Ape "flashed" its 12-inch penis at two
Swedish tourists near his RV park.
Wireless Flash (12 Feb. 2003)

22 Feb. 2003
unnamed
east of Caryville, Washington Co.
Motorist saw a muscular 7-foot primate, 250–275 pounds, with reddish hair,
cross Interstate 10 at 5:30 a.m.
BFRO #5884

Nov. 2003
"J. W."
St. Augustine
Resident walking a dog on Old Moultrie Rd. saw a black hairy biped, 7–8 feet tall.
BFE

2004
unnamed
Polk Co.
Woman reported seeing a foul-smelling primate.
OS (1 April 2005)

18 Jan. 2004
unnamed
near Ft. Drum, Okeechobee Co.
Motorist saw a "small hominid" 3–4 feet tall, 75–100 pounds, leap over road-side fence and cross U.S. Highway 41 North at 5:30 p.m.
BFRO #7904

14 Feb. 2004
unnamed
rural Bay Co.
Resident heard "almost human" howling sounds before dawn. "Wet dog" smells reported on other occasions.
GCBRO

Spring 2004
2 unnamed
near Ft. Myers
Men clearing brush near State Rd. 80 heard whooping sounds from woods.
BFRO #9885

16 May 2004
unnamed
rural Hillsborough Co.
Camper reported a daylight sighting of a primate 7–8 feet tall with reddish brown hair, resembling "a very tall orangutan."
GCBRO

Aug. 2004
unnamed
Bardin
"Several" sightings reported. One person claimed an auto collision with unknown primate.
BFE

Aug. 2004
Jennifer Ward

Green Swamp, near Ocala
Motorist saw a primate 6–8 feet tall beside highway.
Lakeland Ledger (13 Nov. 2004); OSS (20 Nov. 2004)

8 Aug. 2004
unnamed
south of Greenhead, Washington Co.
Nocturnal sighting of a primate 7–8 feet tall in a farmer's yard, under flood-lights. Same witness reports occasional screams from surrounding woods. Neighbors have found livestock mutilated.
BFRO #9174

6 Sept. 2004
5 unnamed
near Ocklawaha, Marion Co.
Rural residents roused at 6:15 a.m. by "awful smell" and tapping on window. Outside, they saw two hairy bipeds, one 8 feet tall and 400 pounds, the other 6–7 feet tall.
BFRO #9282

20 Nov. 2004
unnamed
rural Lee Co.
GCBRO member hears two "very distinct hoots" from the forest.
GCBRO

June 2005
Scott Marlowe
Polk Co.
During production of a Discovery Channel documentary, witness claimed a Skunk Ape threw a stick and "beaned" him, drawing blood.
TD (14 Aug. 2005)

27 July 2005
unnamed
rural Holmes Co.
Motorist observed an unknown, tailless quadruped cross a woodland road at 6:15 a.m. Reported to GCBRO as a Skunk Ape sighting, despite its lack of resemblance to a primate.
GCBRO

14 Jan. 2006
unnamed
near Osteen
Deer hunter found 3-toed tracks 8 inches long and 2–3 inches deep in soil where his own tracks were ½-inch deep.
message posted to ForestGiants@yahoogroups.com (16 Jan. 2006)

Date unknown
Bill Arnold
Tate's Hell Swamp, Franklin Co.
Motorist saw an 8-foot primate cross Highway 67 at 6:30 p.m.
TD (14 Aug. 2005)

Date unknown
2 unnamed
near Naples
Nocturnal sighting of a primate 7–8 feet tall, leaving footprints "4–6 inches larger" than a man's size-10 shoe. The next day, searchers found flattened palmettos "like a den," reeking with a "godawful smell."
GCBRO

Notes

Preface: The Crypto-Zoo

1. Loren Coleman and Jerome Clark, *Cryptozoology A to Z,* 15, 75.
2. Michael Newton, *Encyclopedia of Cryptozoology: A Global Guide,* 4.
3. J. Richard Greenwell, "A Classificatory System for Cryptozoology," 4.
4. Bernard Heuvelmans, "What Is Cryptozoology?" 1.

Chapter 1. Uninvited Guests

1. Florida Fish and Wildlife Conservation Commission (hereinafter FWCC), "Florida's Exotic Wildlife."
2. Ibid.
3. Michael Stewart, "Jogger Claims to Have Seen Emu."
4. FWCC, "Florida's Exotic Wildlife."
5. Alicia Caldwell, "Monkey See?"; Sandra Pedicini, "Two Rhesus Sightings Give Wekiwa Visitors a Start."
6. FWCC, "Florida's Exotic Wildlife."
7. Newton, *Encyclopedia,* 205.
8. FWCC, "Florida's Exotic Wildlife."
9. Janet Bord and Colin Bord, *Unexplained Mysteries of the 20th Century,* 362; Newton, *Encyclopedia,* 305–6.
10. Colette Bancroft, "Enter the Dragons"; Carie Call, "Cape Scales Back Monitor Lizards."
11. FWCC, "Florida's Exotic Wildlife."

12. David Fleshler, "Abandoned Burmese Pythons Endangering Everglades"; Alva James-Johnson, "Loose Python Devours 18-Pound Siamese Cat near Miami-Dade Home"; Denise Kalette, "Python Bursts after Trying to Eat Gator"; Curtis Morgan, "Invasion of the Everglades: Giant Snakes Have a New Hangout"; Curtis Morgan, "It's Alien versus Predator in Glades Creature Clash."

13. Jerry Hill, "State Snakes Come in All Sizes, Species."

14. Roger Conant and Joseph T. Collins, *A Field Guide to Reptiles and Amphibians of Eastern and Central North America*, 410; "Three Big Snakes."

15. Conant and Collins, *Field Guide*, 342; "A Big Snake Story."

16. FWCC, "Exotic Freshwater Fishes."

17. Newton, *Encyclopedia*, 374; University of Florida Center for Aquatic and Invasive Plants, "Nonindigenous Fishes in Freshwater Systems."

18. "Shark Mystery."

Chapter 2. Going . . . Going . . . Gone?

1. Newton, *Encyclopedia*, 303–4, 375–76, 458.

2. Ibid., 107–9.

3. Ibid., 515–21.

4. George Eberhart, *Mysterious Creatures: A Guide to Cryptozoology*, 87–88; Newton, *Encyclopedia*, 88.

5. Eberhart, *Mysterious Creatures*; Newton, *Encyclopedia*.

6. FWCC, "Florida's Exotic Wildlife."

7. Eberhart, *Mysterious Creatures*, 252–53; Newton, *Encyclopedia*, 212–13; Rex Springston, "Sightings of Rare Bird Discounted."

8. Eberhart, *Mysterious Creatures*; Newton, *Encyclopedia*; Virginia Smith, "Woodpecker's Rediscovery Leads to 'Sightings'"; Cathy Zollo, "FGCU Professor Proven Right about Woodpecker's Fate."

9. Eberhart, *Mysterious Creatures*; Newton, *Encyclopedia*.

10. Cornell University News Service, "Long Thought Extinct, Ivory-Billed Woodpecker Rediscovered in Big Woods of Arkansas."

11. Smith, "Woodpecker's Rediscovery"; Springston, "Sightings"; Zollo, "FGCU Professor."

12. James Lazell Jr., "The Search for Rare Animals: Statistics and Probability."

13. Eberhart, *Mysterious Creatures*, 512–13; Karl Shuker, *In Search of Prehistoric Survivors*, 123–24.

14. Shuker, *In Search*; Eberhart, *Mysterious Creatures*.

15. Shuker, *In Search*, 124–26.

Chapter 3. Leviathans

1. Newton, *Encyclopedia*, 167–69, 416–18.

2. Bernard Heuvelmans, *In the Wake of the Sea Serpents*, 539–69; Loren Cole-

man and Patrick Huyghe, *The Field Guide to Lake Monsters, Sea Serpents, and Other Mystery Denizens of the Deep,* 40–45.

3. Heuvelmans, *In the Wake,* 230–31, 578.

4. Ibid., 557–63, 578.

5. Quoted in ibid., 130–31.

6. Ibid.

7. Ibid., 124–25, 131, 587; Florida Museum of Natural History, "Ichthyology."

8. Heuvelmans, *In the Wake,* 545–46, 581.

9. Ibid., 463–64.

10. Ibid., 464, 583.

11. Quoted ibid., 470.

12. Ibid.

13. Ibid., 471, 543, 584; Newton, *Encyclopedia,* 306.

14. Tim Dinsdale, *Monster Hunt,* 93; William Gibbons and Kent Hovind, *Claws, Jaws, and Dinosaurs,* 27.

15. Dinsdale, *Monster Hunt,* 93–94.

16. Ibid.; Heuvelmans, *In the Wake,* 524–25; TrueAuthority.com, "Death at Sea: Pensacola Harbor."

17. Heuvelmans, *In the Wake,* 525; Gibbons and Hovind, *Claws,* 27; Kent Hovind, "Dr. Hovind's 'Creation Seminar': Part 3b: Dinosaurs Alive Today"; TrueAuthority.com, "Death at Sea."

18. Gibbons and Hovind, *Claws,* 27; Hovind, "Creation Seminar."

19. Diana Harris, "Small Town Stories from the 1960s."

20. Diana Harris, correspondence with author, January 26, 2006; Australian Museum Fish Site, "Oarfish."

21. Thomas Helm, *Shark! Unpredictable Killer of the Sea,* 189.

22. Richard Ellis, *Great White Shark,* 48–67.

23. Ibid., 38; Florida Museum of Natural History, "Ichthyology"; Newton, *Encyclopedia,* 85–87.

24. Heuvelmans, *In the Wake,* 550–57, 562–64, 578, 583, 584.

Chapter 4. *Octopus giganteus*

1. Coleman and Huyghe, *Field Guide to Lake Monsters,* 243; Richard Ellis, *Monsters of the Sea,* 303; Bernard Heuvelmans, *The Kraken and the Colossal Octopus,* 274; Roy Mackal, *Searching for Hidden Animals: An Enquiry in to Zoological Mysteries,* 36–37.

2. Quoted in Heuvelmans, *Kraken,* 273.

3. Ellis, *Monsters,* 304; Heuvelmans, *Kraken,* 273–74; Mackal, *Searching,* 37.

4. Ellis, *Monsters,* 303–4; Heuvelmans, *Kraken,* 276.

5. Ellis, *Monsters,* 304; Heuvelmans, *Kraken,* 274; Mackal, *Searching,* 40.

6. Heuvelmans, *Kraken;* Mackal, *Searching,* 40.

7. Coleman and Huyghe, *Field Guide to Lake Monsters*, 244; Ellis, *Monsters*, 306; Heuvelmans, *Kraken*, 275; Mackal, *Searching*, 38.

8. Ellis, *Monsters;* Heuvelmans, *Kraken;* Mackal; *Searching*, 40–42.

9. Ellis, *Monsters*.

10. Ibid., 307.

11. Ibid.

12. Ibid., 307–8; Heuvelmans, *Kraken*.

13. Ellis, *Monsters*, 307; Heuvelmans, *Kraken*.

14. Quoted in Ellis, *Monsters*, 308–9.

15. Ibid.

16. Ibid., 309–10, 319; Heuvelmans, *Kraken*, 275–76.

17. Heuvelmans, *Kraken*, 275–76.

18. Ellis, *Monsters*, 310–11; Mackal, *Searching*, 42–43.

19. Ellis, *Monsters*, 311; Mackal, *Searching*, 43–45; Forrest Wood and Joseph Gennaro, "An Octopus Trilogy."

20. Roy Mackal, "Biochemical Analyses of Preserved *Octopus giganteus* Tissue"; Mackal, *Searching*, 32–49; Gary Mangiacopra, "*Octopus giganteus* Verrill: A New Species of Cephalopod"; Wood and Gennaro, "Octopus Trilogy."

21. Sidney Pierce, Gerald Smith Jr., Timothy Maugel, and Eugenie Clark, "On the Giant Octopus *(Octopus giganteus)* and the Bermuda Blob: Homage to A. E. Verrill"; Michel Raynal, "Debunking the Debunkers of the Giant Octopus."

22. Mackal, *Searching*, 46.

23. Coleman and Huyghe, *Field Guide to Lake Monsters*, 247–48.

24. Eberhart, *Mysterious Creatures*, 303; Heuvelmans, *Kraken*, 278–79; Mackal, *Searching*, 45–49; Bruce Wright, "The Lusca of Andros."

25. Coleman and Huyghe, *Field Guide to Lake Monsters*, 241–42; "Giant Octopus Blamed for Deep Sea Fishing Disruptions."

26. Coleman and Huyghe, *Field Guide to Lake Monsters*, 242.

27. Eberhart, *Mysterious Creatures*, 206–7.

28. Ibid., 206; Mackal, "Biochemical Analyses."

29. Eberhart, *Mysterious Creatures*.

30. Ibid.; Heuvelmans, *Kraken*, 279.

31. Eberhart, *Mysterious Creatures*, 205–6.

Chapter 5. Freshwater Phantoms

1. Coleman and Huyghe, *Field Guide to Lake Monsters*, 271–73, 312–20.

2. Loren Coleman, *Mysterious America*, 311; John Kirk, *In the Domain of the Lake Monsters*, 298; Newton, *Encyclopedia*, 248.

3. Mackal, *Searching*, 220–21; Coleman, *Mysterious America,* 309–11; Bord and Bord, *Unexplained Mysteries*, 306–97; Betty Garner, *Monster! Monster!*

179–85; Kirk, *In the Domain*, 293–303; Eberhart, *Mysterious Creatures*, 655–90; Coleman and Huyghe, *Field Guide to Lake Monsters*, 305–40.

4. Bord and Bord, *Unexplained Mysteries*, 361; Coleman, *Mysterious America*, 309; Coleman and Huyghe, *Field Guide to Lake Monsters*, 313; Eberhart, *Mysterious Creatures*, 681; Kirk, *In the Domain*, 295.

5. Bord and Bord, *Unexplained Mysteries*, 361; Coleman, *Mysterious America*, 309; Coleman and Huyghe, *Field Guide to Lake Monsters*, 313; Eberhart, *Mysterious Creatures*, 681; Kirk, *In the Domain*, 295.

6. Anonymous untitled article in the *Chester (Pa.) Daily Times*, October 25, 1881.

7. "Mammoth Sea Serpent."

8. Mike Archer, "Old Town by River Holds Rich, Wise History."

9. Shuker, *In Search*, 37; Ivan Sanderson, "The Five Weirdest Wonders of the World."

10. Mark Hall, "Pinky, the Forgotten Dinosaur"; Steve Reudiger, "Pink 'Sea Monster' Lurks in River, Rattles Fishermen."

11. Hall, "Pinky"; Shuker, *In Search*, 37–40; Eberhart, *Mysterious Creatures*, 436–37.

12. Eberhart, *Mysterious Creatures*, 681.

13. "Residents Say There Is Something 'Fishy' in Their Lake"; Karl Shuker, "Alien Zoo."

14. "Residents Say There Is Something 'Fishy,'"

Chapter 6. Old Three-Toes

1. Sanderson, "Five Weirdest Wonders," 27–33.

2. Ibid., 34.

3. Mike Dash, *Borderlands*, 273; Sanderson, "Five Weirdest Wonders," 34.

4. Sanderson, "Five Weirdest Wonders," 34.

5. Ibid., 36.

6. Ibid., 36–37.

7. Ibid., 37.

8. Ibid., 37–38.

9. Ibid., 35.

10. Newton, *Encyclopedia*, 410.

11. William Moriaty, "La Floridiana: 'There's a Monster on the Beach'"; Sanderson, "Five Weirdest Wonders," 34.

12. Sanderson, "Five Weirdest Wonders," 40–43.

13. Ibid., 43.

14. Ibid., 50.

15. Ibid., 43, 45.

16. Ibid., 38.

17. Ibid., 53–55.

18. Jan Kirby, "Clearwater Can Relax: Monster Is Unmasked"; Dash, *Borderlands*, 275.

19. Dash, *Borderlands*, 275.

20. Ibid.

21. Ibid.; Kirby, "Clearwater"; Bob Rickard, "Florida's Penguin Panic."

22. Newton, *Encyclopedia*, 336–37.

23. Shuker, *In Search*, 87–88; Richard Smith, "The Classic Wilson Nessie Photo: Is the Hoax a Hoax?"

24. Ian Dow, "Legend of a Big Fib"; Newton, *Encyclopedia*, 480–81.

25. Janet Bord and Colin Bord, *The Bigfoot Casebook*; Loren Coleman, *Bigfoot! The True Story of Apes in America*; Newton, *Encyclopedia*.

Chapter 7. Alien Big Cats

1. Newton, *Encyclopedia*, 16–17; Karl Shuker, *Mystery Cats of the World*, 26.

2. Tony Britt, "Jaguarundi Lurking on Florida Soil?"; FWCC, "Florida's Exotic Wildlife."

3. FWCC, "Florida Panther Net."

4. "Escaped Fla. Panther Found Dead on Road"; "Motorist Reports Seeing Panther in East Arlington"; Gabriel Margasak, "Which Wildcat Stalking Area?"; Jordan Kahn, "Tales Suggest This May Still Be Panther Country"; Dan DeWitt, "A Debate over Zoning Brings Out the Big Cat"; J. Christopher Hain, "Mysterious Predator Prevails in the Acreage."

5. Lance Gay, "Discovery of Dead Panther Has Biologists Asking Questions."

6. Newton, *Encyclopedia*, 27; Shuker, *Mystery Cats*, 163–65.

7. Coleman, *Mysterious America*, 115–16, 293; John Lutz and Linda Lutz, "Century-Old Mystery Rises from Shadows," 31; Margasak, "Which Wildcat?"; Newton, *Encyclopedia*, 115.

8. Newton, *Encyclopedia*, 115–17; Shuker, *Mystery Cats*, 160–65.

9. Coleman, *Mysterious America*, 134, 155, 295.

10. "Lion on the Loose Could Be Wild Goose Chase."

11. Coleman, *Mysterious America*, 150–59, 292–96.

12. Shuker, *Mystery Cats*, 170–72; Coleman, *Mysterious America*, 153–54, 159, 292–96.

Chapter 8. Missing Links

1. Eberhart, *Mysterious Creatures*, 167; Newton, *Encyclopedia*, 430–31.

2. John Green, *Sasquatch: The Apes among Us*; Bord and Bord, *Bigfoot Casebook*; Rick Berry, *Bigfoot on the East Coast*; Bigfoot Field Researchers Organization (hereinafter BFRO); Gulf Coast Bigfoot Research Organization (hereinafter GCBRO).

3. Berry, *Bigfoot;* BFRO; Bigfoot Encounters, "Florida" (hereinafter Bigfoot Encounters); Bord and Bord, *Bigfoot Casebook;* GCBRO.

4. Chad Arment, *The Historical Bigfoot*, 123–25; Berry, *Bigfoot;* BFRO; Bigfoot Encounters; Bord and Bord, *Bigfoot Casebook;* GCBRO.

5. Anonymous untitled article, *Edinburgh (Scotland) Advertiser*, July 21, 1818; Bord and Bord, *Bigfoot Casebook*, 151.

6. Anonymous untitled article, *August (Maine) Daily Kennebec Journal*, July 12, 1872.

7. "Bloodhounds Fear."

8. Berry, *Bigfoot*, 77; Bigfoot Encounters.

9. Berry, *Bigfoot*, 77; BFRO, report 4795; Bord and Bord, *Bigfoot Casebook*, 160; Bord and Bord, *Unexplained Mysteries*, 362; Green, *Sasquatch*, 271.

10. Berry, *Bigfoot*, 77; Bord and Bord, *Bigfoot Casebook*, 162; Bord and Bord, *Unexplained Mysteries*, 362; Cryptozoology; Green, *Sasquatch*, 271–72.

11. Cryptozoology.

12. Berry, *Bigfoot*, 77–79; BFRO; GCBRO.

13. Berry, *Bigfoot*, 77–79; BFRO, report 723; Bord and Bord, *Bigfoot Casebook*, 171, 173; Bord and Bord, *Unexplained Mysteries*, 362; Cryptozoology; Green, *Sasquatch*, 272; John Keel, *The Complete Guide to Mysterious Beings*, 110; Philip Rife, *Bigfoot across America*, 62.

14. Berry, *Bigfoot*, 77–78; Bord and Bord, *Bigfoot Casebook*, 168; Bord and Bord, *Unexplained Mysteries*, 362; Keel, *Complete Guide*, 109–10; Mark Pino, "'Horror' Story No Fool's Prank from '66 Vault"; Rife, *Bigfoot across America*, 61–62.

15. Berry, *Bigfoot*, 77–78; Bord and Bord, *Bigfoot Casebook*, 172–74; Bord and Bord, *Unexplained Mysteries*, 362; Eberhart, *Mysterious Creatures*, 392.

16. Berry, *Bigfoot*, 77, 79; Bigfoot Encounters; Bord and Bord, *Bigfoot Casebook*, 187; BFRO, report 445; Place Names, "Florida."

17. Berry, *Bigfoot*, 78; Bord and Bord, *Bigfoot Casebook*, 182–83; Bord and Bord, *Unexplained Mysteries*, 362.

18. GCBRO.

19. Berry, *Bigfoot*, 79; Bigfoot Encounters; BFRO, report 6692; Cryptozoology; "The Skunk Ape over the Years."

20. Berry, *Bigfoot*, 79; Cryptozoology.

21. Berry, *Bigfoot*, 79; Bord and Bord, *Bigfoot Casebook*, 184, 187; Bord and Bord, *Unexplained Mysteries*, 362; Eberhart, *Mysterious Creatures*, 505; Green, *Sasquatch*, 272–73; Loren Coleman, "Talk about Myths."

22. Berry, *Bigfoot*, 79–92; BFRO, reports 115, 414, 592, 1021, 1030, 1608, 1719, 2657, 2856, 5369, 5519, 7205, 7627; Bord and Bord, *Bigfoot Casebook*, 117, 121, 131–32, 188, 199, 201, 203–7, 209, 211–13, 215, 218; Coleman, *Bigfoot!* 162; Coleman, *Mysterious America*, 216; Cryptozoology; GCBRO; Green, *Sasquatch*, 273, 276–80; Rife, *Bigfoot across America*, 64–66.

23. Berry, *Bigfoot*, 79–90; Bigfoot Encounters; BFRO, report 7627.

24. Berry, *Bigfoot*, 81, 82, 85, 88; BFRO, report 414; Bigfoot Encounters.

25. Berry, *Bigfoot*, 80, 82, 86; BFRO, report 414; Bigfoot Encounters.

26. Berry, *Bigfoot*, 82, 84, 85; Bigfoot Encounters.

27. Berry, *Bigfoot*, 82–85, 87, 88; BFRO, report 414; "Big Foot Reported Treading South"; GCBRO; "Lurking Bigfoot Trick or Treat?"

28. Berry, *Bigfoot*, 79, 86, 89–91; Bigfoot Encounters; "Lurking Bigfoot Trick or Treat?"

29. Bigfoot Encounters; Green, *Sasquatch*, 280.

30. Berry, *Bigfoot*, 93; Bigfoot Encounters; BFRO; Cryptozoology; GCBRO; "Police Think Mystery Footprints Are Fakes"; Rife, *Bigfoot across America*, 66–67.

31. Berry, *Bigfoot*, 93; BFRO, report 2566.

32. Berry, *Bigfoot*, 93; BFRO, report 5510; GCBRO; "Police Think Mystery Footprints Are Fakes."

33. BFRO, report 1275.

34. Tom Bayles, "It's Big, It's Hairy, It's Skunk Ape"; BFRO; Bigfoot Encounters; Cryptozoology; Eberhart, *Mysterious Creatures*, 505–6; GCBRO; Leslie Roberts, "The Legend of the Skunk Ape"; Eric Tiansay, "Panther Tracker Claims Bigfoot Sighting"; Cyril Zaneski and Susan Cocking, "Mysterious 'Ape' Raising a Big Stink."

35. BFRO, report 720.

36. Bayles, "It's Big"; BFRO, report 721; Cryptozoology; Eberhart, *Mysterious Creatures*, 505–6; "Everglades Residents Report Sightings of Skunk Ape"; Roberts, "Legend"; Zaneski and Cocking, "Mysterious 'Ape.'"

37. Christine Barretta, "Skunktober Fest"; Bayles, "It's Big"; Bigfoot Encounters; BFRO, report 634; Malcolm Brabant, "Ape Tape Divides Experts"; Cryptozoology; "Everglades Residents Report Sightings of Skunk Ape"; GCBRO; Green, *Sasquatch;* Michael McCormack, "Skunk Ape: Shealy Claims to Have New Photos of Elusive Legend"; Roberts, "Legend"; "The Skunk Ape over the Years"; Tiansay, "Panther Tracker"; Elizabeth Wendt, "Miami PBS Station Films Skunk Ape–Seeking Expedition"; Elizabeth Wendt-Kellar, "Shealy Sighting"; Zaneski and Cocking, "Mysterious 'Ape.'"

38. BFRO, reports 731, 733, 736, 1407.

39. BFRO, reports 446, 598, 2848, 2915, 5702, 5884, 7904, 9113, 9174, 9282, 9885; Bigfoot Encounters; Cindy Crawford, "Area Has Its Share of Unexplained Happenings"; Eberhart, *Mysterious Creatures*, 506; Linda Florea, "Woman Says 'Skunk Ape' Stood Up beside Highway"; GCBRO; Stephen Wagner, "Smelly Bigfoot: The Skunk Ape."

40. Newton, *Encyclopedia*, 317.

41. Coleman, *Bigfoot!* 150–57; Tom Lyons, "News Conspiracy Smells Like Mysterious 'Skunk Ape'"; Chester Moore Jr., "X-Files: Alleged 'Skunk Ape'

Baffles Experts"; Newton, *Encyclopedia,* 317; Steve Otto, "Absolute Kinda Irrefutable Proof of Skunk Ape."

42. BFRO, reports 446, 5702, 5884, 7904; GCBRO.

43. Berry, *Bigfoot,* 82; Newton, *Encyclopedia,* 196–97, 286, 315, 481–82.

44. Newton, *Encyclopedia,* 62.

45. BFRO, report 5510; Newton, *Encyclopedia,* 62, 199.

46. BFRO, report 1021; GCBRO; Kathleen Laufenberg, "Florida's Monster."

47. Defenders of Wildlife, "Florida's Imperiled Bears"; Robert Sargent Jr., "The Mystery of the Bald Bears"; "Skunk Ape Flashings Arousing Attention in Everglades."

48. Ivan Sanderson, *Abominable Snowmen: Legend Come to Life,* 94; Eberhart, *Mysterious Creatures,* 506; FWCC, "Florida's Exotic Wildlife."

49. Newton, *Encyclopedia,* 171–72.

50. Loren Coleman and Patrick Huyghe, *The Field Guide to Bigfoot, Yeti, and Other Mystery Primates Worldwide;* Mark Hall, *Living Fossils: The Survival of* Homo gardarensis, *Neandertal Man, and* Homo erectus; Mark Hall, *The Yeti, Bigfoot and True Giants;* Sanderson, *Abominable Snowmen.*

Chapter 9. Stranger Still

1. Eberhart, *Mysterious Creatures,* 47; Mark Hall, *Thunderbirds: The Living Legend;* Mark Hall, correspondence with author, September 7, 2005.

2. Hall, *Thunderbirds,* 93–95; Eberhart, *Mysterious Creatures,* 48–49; Newton, *Encyclopedia,* 456–57.

3. Cryptozoology; Mark Renz, "Ancient Florida: Our 30,000,000 Year Journey."

4. "Snake 35 Feet Long with Wings."

5. Odell Shepard, *The Lore of the Unicorn,* 98–99.

6. Ibid., 99; Eberhart, *Mysterious Creatures,* 568.

7. "A Mermaid at Last."

8. Ibid.

9. Conant and Collins, *Field Guide,* 142–45; FWCC, "Florida's Exotic Wildlife."

10. Eberhart, *Mysterious Creatures,* 435.

11. Coleman, *Mysterious America,* 160–87; Newton, *Encyclopedia,* 223–24.

12. Chad Arment, "Florida 'Kangaroo.'"

13. Coleman, *Mysterious America;* FWCC "Florida's Exotic Wildlife."

14. Brad LaGrange, "Giant Armadillos in Florida?"

15. Ibid.; FWCC, "Florida's Exotic Wildlife."

16. Newton, *Encyclopedia,* 102–3.

17. Scott Corrales, *Chupacabras and Other Mysteries,* 129–30; Eberhart, *Mysterious Creatures,* 106.

18. Eberhart, *Mysterious Creatures,* 106–9; Newton, *Encyclopedia,* 102–5.

Conclusion: Where Be Monsters?

1. Coleman and Clark, *Cryptozoology*, 16; Newton, *Encyclopedia*, 6, 515–21.

2. StateofFlorida.com, "Florida Quick Facts"; Place Names, "Florida"; Adrian Sainz, "Tourists Flocked to Orlando's Attractions."

3. StateofFlorida.com, "Florida Quick Facts."

4. Tina Butler, "Somewhere Out There, Millions of Species Await Discovery"; "New Sea Creatures Discovered"; Newton, *Encyclopedia*, 6.

5. FWCC, "About FWC Law Enforcement"; Awesome Florida! "Florida Facts: Florida Beaches, Vacations, and Information"; StateofFlorida.com, "Florida Quick Facts."

6. FloridaSmart.com, "Florida Lakes and Rivers"; FWCC, "About FWC Law Enforcement"; FWCC, "Florida Lakes (1,000 Acres or Larger)"; Visit Florida.

7. Place Names, "Florida."

8. University of Florida Center for Aquatic and Invasive Plants, "Plant Management in Florida Waters."

9. StateofFlorida.com, "Florida Quick Facts"; Friends of the Everglades; Place Names, "Florida."

10. FloridaEnvironment.com, "Florida Places: The Ocala National Forest"; StateofFlorida.com, "Florida Quick Facts"; FWCC, "About FWC Law Enforcement"; Place Names, "Florida"; Visit Florida.

11. Newton, *Encyclopedia*, 27, 79, 125, 279, 432–33.

12. Ibid., 236.

13. Bernard Heuvelmans, *On the Track of Unknown Animals*, 1–3.

Bibliography

Anonymous. Untitled. *Edinburgh (Scotland) Advertiser,* July 21, 1818.

———. Untitled. *Augusta (Maine) Daily Kennebec Journal,* July 12, 1872.

———. Untitled. *Chester (Pa.) Daily Times,* October 25, 1881.

Archer, Mike. "Old Town by River Holds Rich, Wise History." *Orlando Sentinel,* June 17, 2002.

Arment, Chad. *Cryptozoology: Science and Speculation.* Landisville, Pa.: Coachwhip Publications, 2004.

———. "Florida 'Kangaroo.'" *North American Biofortean Review* 4 (December 2002): 4–5.

———. *The Historical Bigfoot.* Landisville, Pa.: Coachwhip Publications, 2006.

Australian Museum Fish Site. "Oarfish." http://www.amonline.net.au/FISHES/fishfacts/fish/rglesne.htm (accessed February 3, 2006).

Awesome Florida! "Florida Facts: Florida Beaches, Vacations, and Information." http://www.awesomeflorida.com/faqs.htm (accessed November 9, 2005).

Bancroft, Colette. "Enter the Dragons." *St. Petersburg Times,* September 26, 2003.

Barretta, Christine. "Skunktober Fest." *Marco Island (Fla.) Sun-Times,* October 6, 2005.

Bayles, Tom. "It's Big, It's Hairy, It's Skunk Ape." *Tallahassee Democrat,* September 7, 1977.

Berry, Rick. *Bigfoot on the East Coast.* Harrisonburg, Va.: Rick Berry, 1993.

Bigfoot Encounters. "Florida." http://www.n2.net/prey/bigfoot/ (accessed July 18, 2005).

Bigfoot Field Researchers Organization. "Florida." http://www.bfro.net/GDB/ state_listing.asp?state=fl (accessed July 18, 2005).

"Big Foot Reported Treading South." *Ocala Star-Banner,* November 19, 1977.

"A Big Snake Story." *Gettysburg (Pa.) Compiler,* September 18, 1887.

"Bloodhounds Fear." *Davenport (Iowa) Daily Leader,* September 28, 1900.

Bord, Janet, and Colin Bord. *The Bigfoot Casebook.* Harrisburg, Pa.: Stackpole Books, 1982.

———. *Unexplained Mysteries of the 20th Century.* Chicago: Contemporary Books, 1989.

Brabant, Malcolm. "Ape Tape Divides Experts." *BBC News,* July 21, 2000.

Britt, Tony. "Jaguarundi Lurking on Florida Soil?" *Lake City Reporter,* August 29, 2004.

Butler, Tina. "Somewhere Out There, Millions of Species Await Discovery." Mongabay.com, May 17, 2005. http://news.mongabay.com/2005/0517-tina_ butler.html (accessed May 19, 2005).

Caldwell, Alicia. "Monkey See?" *Orlando Sentinel,* November 16, 2003.

Call, Carie. "Cape Scales Back Monitor Lizards." *Fort Meyers News-Press,* June 26, 2004.

Cardinal, Florence. "Florida's Hairy Ape." Suite 101.com, January 27, 2002. http://www.suite101.com/article.cfm/mysterious_creatures/88784 (accessed September 21, 2005).

Churba, Jerry. "Feedback Forum." *Marco Island Sun Times,* January 13, 2005.

C. K. "South Florida's Skunk Ape." Bigfoot Encounters. http://www.n2.net/prey/ bigfoot/creatures/florida.htm (accessed July 18, 2005).

Clark, Forrest. "Four Corners: If You're Looking to Get Scared, Then Look No Further Than Green Swamp." *Lakeland Ledger,* October 28, 2004.

Clark, Jerome. *Unnatural Phenomena.* Santa Barbara, Calif.: ABC-CLIO, 2005.

Coleman, Loren. *Bigfoot! The True Story of Apes in America.* New York: Paraview Pocket Books, 2003.

———. *Mothman and Other Curious Encounters.* New York: Paraview Press, 2002.

———. *Mysterious America.* Rev. ed. New York: Paraview Press, 2001.

———. "Talk about Myths." *Bradenton Herald,* February 22, 2001.

Coleman, Loren, and Jerome Clark. *Cryptozoology A to Z.* New York: Fireside, 1999.

Coleman, Loren, and Patrick Huyghe. *The Field Guide to Bigfoot, Yeti, and Other Mystery Primates Worldwide.* New York: Avon, 1999.

———. *The Field Guide to Lake Monsters, Sea Serpents, and Other Mystery Denizens of the Deep.* New York: Tarcher/Penguin, 2003.

Conant, Roger, and Joseph T. Collins. *A Field Guide to Reptiles and Amphibians of Eastern and Central North America.* 3d ed., expanded. Peterson Field Guide Series. New York: Houghton Mifflin, 1998.

Cornell University News Service. "Long Thought Extinct, Ivory-Billed Wood-pecker Rediscovered in Big Woods of Arkansas." April 28, 2005. http://www.news.cornell.edu/stories/April05/ivorybill.html (accessed February 5, 2007).

Corrales, Scott. *Chupacabras and Other Mysteries*. Murfreesboro, Tenn.: Green-leaf Publications, 1997.

Crawford, Cindy. "Area Has Its Share of Unexplained Happenings." *Daytona Beach News-Journal*, October 5, 2003.

"Creature Sighted." *Superior (Wis.) Evening Telegram*, November 15, 1977.

Cryptozoology. http://members.tripod.com/~UNX3/crypto.html (accessed September 21, 2005).

Dash, Mike. *Borderlands*. Woodstock, N.Y.: Overlook Press, 2000.

Defenders of Wildlife. "Florida's Imperiled Bears." http://www.defenders.org/bearaware/florida/bears.html (accessed October 31, 2005).

DeWitt, Dan. "A Debate over Zoning Brings Out the Big Cat." *St. Petersburg Times*, August 12, 2004.

Dinsdale, Tim. *Monster Hunt*. Washington: Acropolis Books, 1972.

Dow, Ian. "Legend of Big Fib." *Glasgow (Scotland) Daily Record*, December 7, 2002.

Eberhart, George. *Mysterious Creatures: A Guide to Cryptozoology*. Santa Barbara: ABC-CLIO, 2002.

Ellis, Richard. *Great White Shark*. Stanford, Calif.: Stanford University Press, 1991.

———. *Monsters of the Sea*. New York: Alfred A. Knopf, 1994.

"Escaped Fla. Panther Found Dead on Road." Associated Press, March 12, 2003.

"Everglades Residents Report Sightings of Skunk Ape." *Fort Myers News Press*, July 23, 1997.

Fleshler, David. "Abandoned Burmese Pythons Endangering Everglades." *Ft. Lauderdale Sun-Sentinel*, May 13, 2004.

Florea, Linda. "Encounter with a 'Skunk Ape.'" *Orlando Sentinel*, November 26, 2004.

———. "Quest for the Swamp Ape." *Orlando Sentinel*, September 4, 2005.

———. "Woman Says 'Skunk Ape' Stood Up beside Highway." *Orlando Sentinel*, November 20, 1984.

FloridaEnvironment.com. "Florida Places: The Ocala National Forest," July 23, 2001. http://www.floridaenvironment.com/programs/fe10723.htm (accessed September 19, 2005).

Florida Fish and Wildlife Conservation Commission. "About FWC Law Enforce-ment." http://myfwc.com/law/aboutus.htm (accessed October 5, 2005).

———. "Exotic Freshwater Fishes." http://floridafisheries.com/Fishes/non-native.html (accessed July 18, 2005).

————. "Florida Lakes (1,000 Acres or Larger)." http://floridafisheries.com/ docum/lakes.html (accessed October 5, 2005).

————. "Florida Panther Net." http://myfwc.com/panther/ (accessed September 1, 2005).

————. "Florida's Exotic Wildlife." http://www.myfwc.com/critters/exotics/exotics .asp (accessed July 18, 2005).

Florida Museum of Natural History. "Ichthyology." http://www.flmnh.ufl.edu/ fish/Gallery/Descript/baskingshark/baskingshark.html (accessed August 2, 2005).

FloridaSmart.com. "Florida Lakes and Rivers." http://www.floridasmart.com/ sciencenature/naturalflorida/lakesrivers.htm (accessed October 5, 2005).

Friends of the Everglades. http://www.everglades.org (accessed October 5, 2005).

Garner, Betty. *Monster! Monster!* Blaine, Wash.: Hancock House, 1995.

Gay, Lance. "Discovery of Dead Panther Has Biologists Asking Questions." Scripps Howard News Service, July 6, 2005.

"Giant Octopus Blamed for Deep Sea Fishing Disruptions." *ISC Newsletter* 4 (autumn 1985): 1–6.

Gibbons, William, and Kent Hovind. *Claws, Jaws, and Dinosaurs.* Pensacola: CSE Publications, 1999.

Green, John. *Sasquatch: The Apes among Us.* Blaine, Wash.: Hancock House, 1978.

Greenwell, J. Richard. "A Classificatory System for Cryptozoology." *Cryptozoology* 4 (1985): 1–14.

Gulf Coast Bigfoot Research Organization. "Florida." http://gcbro.com/fldb1. htm (accessed July 18, 2005).

Hain, J. Christopher. "Mysterious Predator Prevails in the Acreage." *Palm Beach Post,* November 18, 2004.

Hall, Mark. *Living Fossils: The Survival of* Homo gardarensis, *Neandertal Man, and* Homo erectus. Minneapolis: Mark A. Hall Publications, 1999.

————. "Pinky, the Forgotten Dinosaur." *Wonders* 1, no. 4 (December 1992): 51–59.

————. *Thunderbirds: The Living Legend.* 2d ed. Minneapolis: Mark A. Hall Publications, 1994.

————. *The Yeti, Bigfoot, and True Giants.* Minneapolis: Mark A. Hall Publications, 1997.

Harris, Diana. "Small Town Stories from the 1960s." *Englewood (Fla.) Sun,* January 14, 2006.

Helm, Thomas. *Shark! Unpredictable Killer of the Sea.* New York: Collier Books, 1961.

Heuvelmans, Bernard. *In the Wake of the Sea Serpents.* New York: Hill and Wang, 1968.

————. *The Kraken and the Colossal Octopus.* London: Kegan Paul, 2003.

————. *On the Track of Unknown Animals.* London: Kegan Paul, 1995.

————. "What Is Cryptozoology?" *Cryptozoology* 1 (1982): 1–12.

Hill, Jerry. "Ape Men Sightings Just Tall Tales." *Bradenton Herald,* February 14, 2001.

————. "State Snakes Come in All Sizes, Species." *Bradenton Herald,* January 12, 2005.

————. "Stories of 'Skunk Apes' Are Dubious." *Bradenton Herald,* July 10, 2002.

Hovind, Kent. "Dr. Hovind's 'Creation Seminar': Part 3b: Dinosaurs Alive Today." http://www.algonet.se/~tourtel/hovind_seminar/seminar_part3b.html (accessed August 2, 2005).

Hurtley, Michelle. "Not Nemo—Very Rare Oarfish Found on Marco Beach." *Marco Island Sun Times,* February 5, 2004.

"In Search of the Skunk Ape." *Orlando Sentinel* (September 6, 2003).

James-Johnson, Alva. "Loose Python Devours 18-Pound Siamese Cat near Miami-Dade Home." *Fort Lauderdale Sun-Sentinel,* October 10, 2005.

Kahn, Jordan. "Tales Suggest This May Still Be Panther Country." *Daytona Beach News-Journal,* May 23, 2004.

Kalette, Denise. "Python Bursts after Trying to Eat Gator." Associated Press, October 5, 2005.

Keel, John. *The Complete Guide to Mysterious Beings.* New York: Doubleday, 1994.

Kirby, Jan. "Clearwater Can Relax: Monster Is Unmasked." *St. Petersburg Times,* June 11, 1988.

Kirk, John. *In the Domain of the Lake Monsters.* Toronto: Key Porter Books, 1998.

LaGrange, Brad. "Giant Armadillos in Florida?" *North American Biofortean Review* 3 (October 2001): 26–27.

Laufenberg, Kathleen. "Florida's Monster." *Tallahassee Democrat,* August 14, 2005.

Lazell, James, Jr. "The Search for Rare Animals: Statistics and Probability." *Cryptozoology* 5 (1986): 135–38.

"Lion on the Loose Could Be Wild Goose Chase." WFTV Orlando, November 3, 2003.

Lounsberry, Alyse. "Was It Bigfoot? Preacher Says Story No Lie." *Ocala Star-Banner,* November 16, 1977.

"Lurking Bigfoot Trick or Treat?" *Orlando Sentinel Star,* October 5, 1977.

Lutz, John, and Linda Lutz. "Century-old Mystery Rises from the Shadows." *North American Bio-Fortean Review* (October 2001: 30–50).

Lyons, Tom. "News Conspiracy Smells Like Mysterious 'Skunk Ape.'" *Sarasota Herald-Tribune,* February 14, 2001.

Mackal, Roy. "Biochemical Analyses of Preserved *Octopus giganteus* Tissue." *Cryptozoology* 5 (1986): 55–62.

———. *Searching for Hidden Animals: An Enquiry into Zoological Mysteries.* Garden City, N.Y.: Doubleday, 1980.

"Mammoth Sea Serpent." *Atlanta Constitution,* March 29, 1895.

Mangiacopra, Gary. "Another *Octopus giganteus* Rebuttal—Again!" *Of Sea and Shore* 21 (winter 1999): 233–34.

———. "The Great Ones: A Fragmented History of the Giant and Colossal Octopus." *Of Sea and Shore* 7 (summer 1976): 93–96.

———. "More on *Octopus giganteus.*" *Of Sea and Shore* 8 (fall 1977): 174, 178.

———. "*Octopus giganteus* Verrill: A New Species of Cephalopod." *Of Sea and Shore* 6 (spring 1975): 3–10, 51–52.

Mangiacopra, Gary, Michel Raynal, Dwight Smith, and David Avery. Him of the Hairy Hands': *Octopus giganteus* Rebuttal—Again!" *Of Sea and Shore* 21 (winter 1999): 233–34.

———. "*Octopus giganteus:* Still Alive and Hiding Where?" *Of Sea and Shore* 18 (spring 1996): 5–12.

"Man Keeps Florida Skunk Ape Legend Alive." *Bradenton Herald,* May 9, 2005.

Margasak, Gabriel. "Which Wildcat Stalking Area?" *Stuart News,* September 17, 2003.

McCormack, Michael. "Skunk Ape: Shealy Claims to Have New Photos of Elusive Legend." *Naples Daily News,* September 12, 1998.

Meek, Dan. "Skunk Ape Is Skunked." *Everglades Echo,* July 9, 2002.

"A Mermaid at Last." *Marion (Ohio) Daily Star,* May 13, 1890.

Moore, Chester, Jr. "X-Files: Alleged 'Skunk Ape' Baffles Experts." *Orange (Tex.) Leader,* February 22, 2001.

Morgan, Curtis. "Invasion of the Everglades: Giant Snakes Have a New Hangout." *Miami Herald,* December 22, 2002.

———. "It's Alien versus Predator in Glades Creature Clash." *Miami Herald,* October 5, 2005.

Moriaty, William. "La Floridiana: 'There's a Monster on the Beach.'" Nolan's Pop Culture Review, February 18–24, 2002. http://www.crazedfanboy.com/nolansnewsstand02/laflapcr100.html (accessed August 24, 2005).

"Motorist Reports Seeing Panther in East Arlington." WJX-TV Jacksonville, August 18, 2003.

"New Sea Creatures Discovered." *Singapore Straits Times,* June 13, 2005.

Newton, Michael. *Encyclopedia of Cryptozoology: A Global Guide.* Jefferson, N.C.: McFarland, 2005.

Otto, Steve. "Absolute Kinda Irrefutable Proof of Skunk Ape." *Tampa Tribune,* February 13, 2001.

———. "Next on Fox: When Skunk Apes Go Bad." *Tampa Tribune,* February 17, 2001.

Palmer, Tom. "Sightings of 'Swamp Ape' Should Be Noted with Skepticism." *Lakeland Ledger,* January 5, 2005.

Pedicini, Sandra. "Two Rhesus Sightings Give Wekiwa Visitors a Start." *Orlando Sentinel,* June 9, 2002.

Pierce, Sidney, Gerald Smith Jr., Timothy Maugel, and Eugenie Clark. "On the Giant Octopus *(Octopus giganteus)* and the Bermuda Blob: Homage to A. E. Verrill." *Biological Bulletin* 188 (1995): 219–30.

Pino, Mark. "'Horror' Story No Fool's Prank from '66 Vault." *Orlando Sentinel,* April 1, 2005.

Place Names. "Florida." http://www.placenames.com/us/12 (accessed October 5, 2005).

"Police Think Mystery Footprints Are Fakes." *Houston Chronicle,* July 2, 1980.

Raynal, Michel. "The Case for the Giant Octopus." *Fortean Studies* 1 (1994): 210–34.

———. "Debunking the Debunkers of the Giant Octopus." *INFO Journal* no. 74 (winter 1996): 24–27.

———. "Properties of Collagen and the Nature of the Florida Monster." *Cryptozoology* 6 (1987): 129–30.

Renz, Mark. "Ancient Florida: Our 30,000,000 Year Journey." Absolutely Florida. http://www.abfla.com/1tocf/wildlife/armadillos.html (accessed March 21, 2005).

"Residents Say There Is Something 'Fishy' in Their Lake." *Boca Beacon,* August 29, 2003.

Reudiger, Steve. "Pink 'Sea Monster' Lurks in River, Rattles Fishermen." *Jacksonville Times-Union,* May 16, 1975.

Rickard, Bob. "Florida's Penguin Panic." *Fortean Times* 66 (December 1992–January 1993): 41–43.

Rife, Philip. *Bigfoot across America.* Lincoln, Neb.: Writers Club Press, 2000.

Roberts, Leslie. "The Legend of the Skunk Ape." *Lake City Reporter,* September 26, 1997.

Sainz, Adrian. "Tourists Flocked to Orlando's Attractions." *Sarasota Herald-Tribune,* November 8, 2005.

Sanderson, Ivan. *Abominable Snowmen: Legend Come to Life.* Philadelphia: Chilton Books, 1961.

———. "The Five Weirdest Wonders of the World." *Argosy,* November 1968, 21–23, 83–85.

———. *More "Things."* New York: Pyramid Books, 1969.

Sargent, Robert, Jr. "The Mystery of the Bald Bears." *Orlando Sentinel,* December 10, 2002.

Satterfield, Jamie. "New Photo 'Proves' Existence of Everglades 'Skunk Ape.'" *Knoxville (Tenn.) News-Sentinel,* October 13, 1997.

"Shark Mystery." *Ft. Lauderdale Sun-Sentinel,* June 24, 2005.

Shepard, Odell. *The Lore of the Unicorn*. London: George Allen and Unwin, 1930.

Shuker, Karl. "Alien Zoo." *Fortean Times* 178 (January 2004): 26.

———. *In Search of Prehistoric Survivors*. London: Blandford, 1995.

———. *Mystery Cats of the World*. London: Robert Hale, 1989.

"Skunk Ape." Unexplained Mysteries. http://unexplained-mysteries.com/search.php?q=skunk+ape (accessed September 21, 2005).

"Skunk Ape Flashings Arousing Attention in Everglades." *Wireless Flash*, February 12, 2003.

"The Skunk Ape over the Years." *Naples Daily News,* September 22, 2005.

Smith, Richard. "The Classic Wilson Nessie Photo: Is the Hoax a Hoax?" *Fate* 48 (November 1995): 42–44.

Smith, Virginia. "Woodpecker's Rediscovery Leads to 'Sightings.'" *Daytona Beach News-Journal,* May 19, 2005.

"Snake 35 Feet Long with Wings." *Daily Iowa Press,* June 15, 1899.

Springston, Rex. "Sightings of Rare Bird Discounted." *Richmond (Va.) Times-Dispatch,* April 30, 2005.

StateofFlorida.com. "Florida Quick Facts." http://www.stateofflorida.com/Portal/DesktopDefault.aspx?tabid=95 (accessed November 9, 2005).

Stewart, Michael. "Jogger Claims to Have Seen Emu." *Pensacola News Journal,* October 18, 2003.

St. Martin, Tiffany. "Skunk Ape Goes to the Movies." *Naples Daily New,* March 30, 2005.

"Three Big Snakes." *Elyria (Ohio) Republican,* November 14, 1878.

Tiansay, Eric. "Panther Tracker Claims Bigfoot Sighting." *Naples Daily News,* November 20, 1998.

TrueAuthority.com. "Death at Sea: Pensacola Harbor." http://www.trueauthority.com/cryptozoology/death.htm (accessed August 2, 2005).

University of Florida Center for Aquatic and Invasive Plants. "Nonindigenous Fishes in Freshwater Systems." http://aquat1.ifas.ufl.edu/mcfish5.html (accessed July 18, 2005).

———. "Plant Management in Florida Waters." http://plants.ifas.ufl.edu/guide/swamps.html (accessed July 18, 2005).

Verrill, Addison. "Additional Information Concerning the Giant Cephalopod of Florida." *American Journal of Science* 3 (February 1897): 162–63.

———. "The Florida Sea Monster." *American Naturalist* 31 (April 1897): 304–7.

———. "A Gigantic Cephalopod on the Florida Coast." *American Journal of Science* 4 (January 1897): 79.

———. "The Supposed Giant Octopus of Florida: Certainly Not a Cephalopod." *American Journal of Science* 3 (April 1897): 355–56.

Vieira, Mischa. "Tracking Myakka's Wily Skunk Ape." *Bradenton East County Observer,* July 12, 2001.

Visit Florida. http://www.visitflorida.org/index.cfm?fla=web&webpageid=206 (accessed November 9, 2005).

Wagner, Stephen. "Smelly Bigfoot: The Skunk Ape." About: Paranomal Phenomena. http://paranormal.about.com/od/bigfootsasquatch/a/aa112204.htm (accessed September 21, 2005).

Wendt, Elizabeth. "Miami PBS Station Films Skunk Ape–Seeking Expedition." *Naples Daily News,* September 6, 2003.

Wendt-Kellar, Elizabeth. "Shealy Sighting." *Naples Daily News,* September 22, 2005.

"What Stinks?" *Sarasota Herald-Tribune,* February 12, 2001.

White, Gary. "Our Own Loch Ness Monster?" *Lakeland Ledger,* November 13, 2004.

Wood, Forrest, and Joseph Gennaro. "An Octopus Trilogy." *Natural History* 80 (March 1971): 15–24, 84–87.

Wright, Bruce. "The Lusca of Andros." *Atlantic Advocate* 51 (June 1967): 32–39.

Zaneski, Cyril, and Susan Cocking. "Mysterious 'Ape' Raising a Big Stink." *Miami Herald,* July 28, 1997.

Zollo, Cathy. "FGCU Professor Proven Right about Woodpecker's Fate." *Naples Daily News,* May 9, 2005.

Index

11–13; coelacanth, 9–10; rediscovered, 9–11
lizards: iguanas, 3–4; monitors, 4–5
Loch Ness, Scotland, 48, 65
Loxahatchee, Fla., 71
Lucy and Nancy (ship), 20–21
Lutz, John, 70

Mackal, Roy, 43, 44, 50
Madison County, Fla., 76
manatee, 52, 53–54
Manatee County, Fla., 82, 88, 137, 144
Mangiacopra, Gary, 19, 42
Mango, Fla., 69
Marco, Fla., 29
Marion County, Fla., 75, 82, 86, 89, 92, 95, 140, 154, 155, 165
Martin, David, 65
Martin County, Fla., 82
Marx, Ivan, 95–96
Mary Esther, Fla., 163
Matheson Hammock Park, 101
McCleary, Edward, 26–28
Melbourne, Fla., 151
mermaids, 103–4
Miami, Fla., 24, 108, 111, 134, 151; Monkey Jungle, 7; Seaquarium, 17; Snapper Creek, 7
Miami Beach, Fla., 17
Milton, Fla., 147, 154, 162
Mims, Fla., 81, 125, 150
Miramar, Fla., 135
Mokele-mbembe, 9, 10
monkeys, 2
Monroe County, Fla., 82, 89
Moon Lake, Fla., 83, 87, 134, 140, 141
Mullens, Rant, 96
Murdoch, Fla., 80
Myakka River, 28–29
Myakka State Forest, 95, 145, 158

Naples, Fla., 148, 166
Nassau County, Fla., 74
National Audubon Society, 13
New Harmony, Fla., 153

New River Inlet, Fla., 22–23, 29
New Smyrna Beach, Fla., 151, 162
Nobleton, Fla., 83, 141
Nocturnal, Fla., 159
North Ft. Myers, Fla., 81, 122, 137, 140
North Port, Fla., 145, 158

Oak Hill, Fla., 150
Ocala, Fla., 163, 165
Ocala National Forest, 88, 97, 115, 143, 145, 154, 155
Ochopee, Fla., 90, 97, 145, 155, 156, 157, 163
Ocklawaha, Fla., 165
octopus: *Enteroctopus dolfeini,* 46; *E. megalocyathus,* 46; giant, 33–47
Octopus giganteus, 33–47
Okaloosa County, Fla., 89, 92, 154, 163
Okeechobee County, Fla., 13, 92, 95, 164
Okefenokee Swamp, 13, 114
"Old Three-toes," xiii, 56–66
Old Town, Fla., 59, 62
Oneco, Fla., 141, 142, 143, 144
Orange County, Fla., 6, 75, 78, 82, 88, 89, 146
Orlando, Fla., 6, 111, 139, 146, 152
Osceola County, Fla., 78, 79, 88, 89, 91, 92, 113, 122, 156, 157
Osceola National Forest, 97, 115
Osprey, Fla., 153–54
Osteen, Fla., 165

Paisley, Fla., 146
Palatka, Fla., 77, 120
Palm Beach County, Fla., 69, 82, 86, 89, 112, 132, 163
Palm City, Fla., 70
Panama City, Fla., 25
Pasco County, Fla., 75, 78, 79–80, 82, 83, 92, 95, 130, 134, 135, 148, 149
Peace River, 88, 146
Peace River City, Fla., 126
penguins, 62–63
Pensacola, Fla.: emu in, 9; Police Department, 27; sea monster in, 26–28

Michael Newton is a full-time freelance author, with 191 books published since 1977. His previous works on cryptozoology include *Monsters, Mysteries, and Man* (1979) and the *Encyclopedia of Cryptozoology* (2005), which won the American Library Association's 2006 designation as an Outstanding Reference Book. He is a member of the British Columbia Scientific Cryptozoology Club and the International Bigfoot Society.

5-14-08